# MAKING THE MOST
# OF THE LIFE YOU'VE GOT

# MAKING THE MOST OF THE LIFE YOU'VE GOT

## A MANUAL FOR THE NEW MILLENNIUM

### ANNIE WILSON

ROWAN COMMUNICATIONS LIMITED

First published in the UK in 1998 by Rowan Communications Limited, Fourways, Chalford, Westbury, Wilts, BA13 3RE
Fax: (01373) 827988

Cover photographs: Martin Davison
Printed by Whitstable Litho Printers Ltd., Whitstable, Kent

ISBN: 1-902183-00-2

A catalogue record of this book is available from the British Library

# CONTENTS

# CONTENTS

# EXERCISES ON CASSETTE

# Introduction

# *HOW TO READ THIS MANUAL*

In the beginning was the word, and the word was God. That's what many people believe to be the case. However, what we want to establish in this book is that the word sometimes misleads, and indeed has mislead people through the ages, because in the word is much misunderstanding.

In our view what needs to be felt is <u>the idea behind the word</u>. In using words, the idea is often mistakenly thought to be the understanding of the word, rather than the understanding of the idea itself.

What we are maintaining in this book, is that in the idea is an <u>understanding</u> of how the world works. By experiencing the world in an imaginative manner, the world can actually begin to look different to the idea of the world that has come through the endless stream of words that the intellectual man in the street has uttered.

In other words, you and I, those who are not in that hierarchical strata of intellectual society, can actually become acquainted, through the inner eye of the imagination, with the real world behind the world we see.

May we suggest that this book is like a cobblestone street. Each bump in the pathway allows the reader to take a look at what is going on in their lives. They can experience the effect of certain decisions and choices they have made in a living manner – not from an emotional standpoint, but in a way that will take them into a realm of reality not usually experienced in the hubbub of daily life.

May we suggest that you suspend disbelief. That is the number one criterion required to allow this book to work on the inner planes of experience. To become involved with the book takes a certain leap of faith, that the inner eye can be accessed simply by believing that there is a faculty in all of us, that can and will see from the inside, so to speak, as opposed to the outside.

Creating a circle around yourself in your imagination can feel the most important thing in your life to date if you have never felt the inner security of making yourself safe in a circle. This is inner gazing. Feeling what it is like to create in the imagination, so that the inner experience of life is as real and as dynamic as all the outward things you do to get on in life.

What we feel the reader should try to ascertain is <u>how</u> they, uniquely, perceive with that inner eye. Some may feel a sensation in the body that 'informs' them of the issues they are addressing through a particular exercise. Some may 'see' the images dancing in front of them. Some may 'hear' words. What is absolutely certain is that anyone and everyone <u>can</u> access the inner dimensions of their being in some manner.

There is available to everyone a facility to access the inner aspects of the external senses. Believe it or not some people may actually <u>smell</u> their inner dimensional being, and in the sensing of that smell, there is a notion of how the mind can access the meaning of that smell – or sound, or picture – without actually <u>thinking</u> about it.

When information enters through the mind there is a dissociation with the content. There is a sorting and framing that accepts or rejects things because they <u>fit</u> or <u>don't fit</u> a preconceived notion of something. When the body is the receiver of that information, the information itself will alter the body set in such a way that will eventually alter the mind set, which in turn will alter the body's state of mind as it were.

We feel health can be returned to the body in this manner. Rather than treat the symptoms of an illness, there is an inner mechanism that can redress the balance of emotional ill-health, through acknowledgement that the body is the best arbitrator of its own health.

May we ask the reader to completely accept that the book has a pattern and purpose in and of itself. All the exercises, on tape and in the book, need to be taken in a serious manner, as a partnership between you and those unseen beings who want, more than anything else in the world, to help you establish the real essence of mankind.

Make a real effort to make the place where you choose to do the exercises, a 'sacred space'. Light a candle; do a little cleansing of that space. Create a lightness in the room by making a gesture of clearance that makes you feel good.

The exercises repeated on tape are those we feel the reader would prefer to take more time over, and are offered as guided mediations. Relax for several minutes before you play each exercise, and if you need more time to experience what is being said, use the pause button. Remember to bring your consciousness back to the room at the end of each exercise, and feel your feet firmly on the floor, to be fully present.

No matter how tempted you are to skip through from one exercise to another, or to skip an exercise altogether, may we suggest there is an energetic build up that can and will create a changing atmosphere around you. May we ask the reader to try to make it a meditative diary that you read page after page rather than jump from here to there. It will work at many levels but it does need to be read in sequence.

In the heavens are more realities than meet the eye. Each human being has access to greater realities than they could possibly imagine at this stage of evolution. But evolve they will.

Most people have some notion that psychic realities are glamorous and given to only the few bright sparks who inhabit a twilight world of magic and mystery. In fact the psychic faculty is open to all and sundry should they wish to stay at the lower levels of mystery.

However, what we are advocating is a relationship to the Divine aspect of the human being, which takes us beyond the magic and mystery level, into a realm of pure spirit. By feeling those levels within the human body, we link to the Soul aspect of humanity. The soul is the link between human and spiritual realms that takes us way further than merely delving in magic at the lowest levels of instinctual responses.

May we suggest that these spiritual levels of experience are the result of a decision to change from an emotionally self-perpetuating being, to a human being of unique talent and expression. No one should imagine the shift of the times is going to be easy, but if you really respond to the changes in the air, so to speak, you can and will respond magnetically to the changes required of you, to live a full life in the now, in the moment of time you are experiencing YOU, NOW.

No one can respond to the full magnitude of being human until they are able to let go all the issues that hold them into a binding relationship to self that keeps the wheel of karma turning endlessly. When change becomes the focus of the human life and a bid is made to let go karmic patterning, we can begin to understand the nature of life everlasting here on Earth.

Annie Wilson has been able to release sufficiently her karmic, genetic and personal history, in order to create a vortex of energetic resonance within her being. This has allowed her whole experience of life to magnify, opening up a pathway to 'more of the universal mind', and to extra dimensional realities that have been waiting for thousands and thousands of years to return to help mankind make this leap in consciousness.

This is not a unique experience. Many many people are now unfolding like beautiful flowers in their resonance with other realms. The world is a far far bigger place than anyone could possibly imagine. Let it unfold in your life right now.

It's very very simple – if you totally accept that life now, here and now, right now, is as perfect as it's ever likely to get. You just have to recognise it. And so be it.

# Chapter One

# *MAKE YOURSELF READY FOR HAPPINESS*

In the age of the Internet we are given the impression that unless we know exactly what is going on in every aspect of human existence we are missing out on LIFE. In fact that is absolutely untrue. In our view what is essential for the art of living a full and happy life is to <u>understand</u> the meaning of life itself. Note we say understand, not <u>know</u> the meaning of life.

Understanding life is totally different from an endless search to know everything there is to know about life. Science is based on the need to know. Education at this moment is based on the need to know. Happily happiness itself is not based on anyone knowing anything at all, but understanding everything there is to understand.

Understanding is first and foremost an acknowledgement that life is actually based on a totally different premise than that advocated by the paternalistic political systems in the West. In fact, in our view what needs to be understood right now is that understanding was the very first means of communication on the planet. A kind of telepathy made the first human beings able to understand their environment without needing to speak what they knew.

Language came a long time later when commerce became the means of exchanging goods and services. Today we exchange goods and services as a means of making people slaves to the economic system and creating an environment in which people are totally unable to understand the true meaning of life. In many ways language was the cross to bear and the moment when dominance and servility became the dual poles of western thought.

In many ways language has been the undoing of the human race because it has led the idea of commerce to become the sole motivating factor of human reasoning, and therefore of the human need to know in order to become more dominant rather than more servile in the world. Language created the human striving to know more and more in order to become a powerful source against a less powerful opponent. Language became the means by which one man became powerful over another.

We feel the way to combat the real tragedy of language as a means to power is to understand how the human being became so fixed on knowing as opposed to understanding.

*        *        *

In the Spanish Civil War many people fought for the right to let others be free to speak their minds, whatever their doctrine, race or creed. Some of the men and women who decided to fight for the Spanish cause came from the most creditable seats of learning in Britain. What made them want to fight the cause was a true sense that justice had to be seen to be done, and many people gave their lives to what in the end turned out to be a hopeless cause. Why?

Britain has an extremely powerful and innate need to understand justice as the motivating source of leadership. Justice was the reason so many dedicated men and women served in the colonies. Colonial rule was based on truth and justice and a sense of leadership that enabled the British to believe that they were offering these countries the opportunity to make of their countries what Britain had made of hers: decent, upstanding and honest.

Unfortunately when justice without love is the motivation of leadership, there is created an imbalance between 'the haves' and 'have nots' in any situation. Those who are done unto and those who do unto others. Again, the system of leadership based on justice creates a means in which one sector has power over another.

Power over another person has the makings of a kind of energy field that can then only feed on itself and create a web in which the whole of humanity is caught. In our view what we want to imply is that once human beings can understand what is the true nature of life then they can begin to move towards the understanding of happiness. Until then the most powerful indicators of unhappiness, the need to know and a concentration of justice, as opposed to love, as the motivation of life, will mask a truly miraculous understanding of how to be happy in the life you have.

Once the need to know is eradicated, the more important and stimulating relationship to understanding will emerge. While so many people are wanting to know more and more, and submerging their inner relationship to true understanding, then the world will become even more sterile and undernourished, and needing to feed itself on more and more information to feel worthwhile.

In our view once the human being can switch from knowing to understanding, the way to true happiness is assured. There's a promise! Can you begin to grasp the difference between understanding and knowing, in the way we are speaking to you?

Understanding is a way of perceiving the meaning behind, rather than an intellectual grasping of the words we say. It requires a very different 'listening' mechanism to the one where the mind interprets words in a linear fashion. By 'listening' in a non linear way, the words themselves create meaning rather than knowing. May we try an exercise to facilitate this kind of listening?

*First of all, we suggest you make a tape of the words we have already said. Read the words in a slower way than you might normally and say them in a lower tone.*

*Now, let the words play back to you while you sit in a chair with a cushion at your feet, feeling your feet feel cosy and warm nestling on the cushion. Can you do that? Now, listen to the words with your feet! Yes, with your feet! Feeling warm and cosy on the cushion. Is this possible? What happens?*

*Can you sense an understanding of what we are saying in a totally different way to the way you heard the words as you read them?*

Now, since we hope you have <u>heard</u> the words in a different way to the way you <u>read</u> them, may we say again what we meant – in a new way?

Take a cushion and put your feet on the cushion. Test it for warmth and cosiness, and then relax. Now read the next page in this manner.

May we suggest that the most important way to look at a book is to really accept that what is being offered is not the only way in which to understand what is being offered. In our view the most valuable way to read a book is to 'read between the lines', or rather to validate what you read by 'hearing' a completely different subtext going on in your head.

This subtext is an automatic mechanism that allows you to understand in a feeling way what you are being given through language. This mechanism allows you to verify what you are reading by an inner computer that tells you whether or not this information is truly valid for you as an individual. Whether or not the information can add to the infinite number of inputs that enter your sphere of activity daily.

In other words, the inner computer can allow you to experience the words as a living, breathing aspect of who you are and who you are to become. 'Hearing' a book rather than just 'seeing' a book allows you to filter into your atmosphere a truly significant amount of information that can turn into a real understanding of the world around you, not just a verbal, linear piece of information that has no affect on your well-being whatsoever.

We feel the most rewarding kind of books are those that make the person say 'ah ha', in a kind of inner resonance to the words on the page; a resonance within the body almost, that can validate what is being read as a meaningful experience to the person reading. Understanding at a visceral level begins to build up a picture of the world that is whole, complete and manifestly more interesting than the world as it is at present; reduced to the sum total of what people are able to know with the small part of their brains that remembers information.

Understanding life is to truly experience every aspect of it in a visceral, caring and non-competitive way. We can only be non-competitive if the information we are given can be tailor-made, by ourselves, to fit our own identikit picture of who we are and who we are to become.

Information that has to be remembered and applied in the old way leads to such inequality that there will always be the need to establish hierarchies of better and best to impart a verdict on such issues as who can and who cannot wield power through disputably discarnate knowledge.

By discarnate knowledge, we mean information that is unrelated and insignificant to the person who has the knowledge. In some ways the Internet is a marvellous invention because the knowledge is spread far far wider than in different times when knowledge, and power, were in the hands of the few. But in some ways it is also a force for destruction because the more extraneous knowledge there is to know, there is less and less incentive for people to understand in the way we are advocating through personal, intimate experience.

Now, we feel the most important aspect of making clear that

understanding is far more valid than knowing, is that most men are unable to resist flirting with the idea of the Internet now. May we show you what happens when the mind is switched on to information only, and not to experience?

*Picture a toad crossing the road for a moment. Make the toad really slow crossing the road and bring in a car coming down the road at quite a high speed. There is every reason to fear that the toad will be squashed by the car, but also almost as much reason to suppose that the car will not do so because the toad will be positioned in the space between the wheels.*

*Watch the toad carefully now as the car approaches. Make the car break suddenly just ahead of the toad. Watch how the toad begins to speed up to cross the road and allow yourself to feel relieved. Why are you relieved?*

*Make the assumption you prefer the toad to be alive rather than dead and tell us what is in your mind right now. Can we guess? Maybe you're thinking the toad was right to speed up even though the car had stopped. Maybe you felt the car ought to have stopped sooner. Maybe you are thinking another toad might have crossed the road before the other one.*

*Feel what you are feeling, rather than thinking what you are thinking, and write down what that toad makes you feel about it suddenly. Make a note about what the toad makes you feel, not what you think the toad might have done or what the car might have done. Feel the feeling about the toad.*

The story you made up in your head about the toad allows you to understand more about yourself in the space of two minutes than fifty minutes in front of the computer surfing the Internet, doesn't it?

It has put you in touch with making a toad the focus of your attention in order to understand something about yourself that you might not otherwise have known; and understanding about Self is the real clue to understanding about life, and understanding that happiness is the art of understanding, not knowing.

We feel the most valuable thing in the world of human beings is to release a very basic mistake that knowledge is the only way to become a useful human being. Rather, we want to put forward the idea that knowledge is a hindrance to the most important manifestation of humanness and that is an understanding of who and what human beings really are.

Who are they? They are truly the most inventive, creative, magnificent creatures in the universe, if only they would get off the current idea that information is the way to power. Information is the way to paucity of the human spirit which in our view is the only aspect that mankind has not yet fully utilised.

Man can reach the moon but he cannot, to all intents and purposes, understand that he is the moon, that he is the stars, the trees and the firmament. He knows so much, but in fact he understands so little of his potential.

If only he would stop wanting power over others in order to describe himself to the world around him, and begin to delve inside to visit the world inside himself. Then he would never again want to seek dominion over others, but to honour himself in his own dominion, make others alert to his dignity and creativity, and above all, to honour and acknowledge others in theirs.

Making the effort to recognise others as equal is one of the hardest tasks the human race faces. In our view the reason hierarchical life has become such a feature of modern life is that man has become oblivious to his environment. That may sound far fetched but in our view the most important relationship man can have to the environment is one of knowing his own place in that environment is one of equality.

There is no hierarchy in Nature, simply the most beautiful design in which each creature, each plant, each mineral has its place. Man is simply the crowning glory of Nature in that man alone has the facility to nurture his fellow creatures in a manner that allows his particular skill, that of thought, to manifest wisely and magnificently in the service of all. Not, you understand, in the service of greed, self aggrandisement and hierarchical structures of power.

May we add here that in our view manifestation of wisdom depends entirely on the understanding that man (and we aways mean as in man and woman) is a manifold creature, spiritually, emotionally, physically and mentally. Man needs to understand that he is the pivotal point in evolutionary history, a guardian of this planet rather than its master and slave to desires that manifestly upset the balance of not only the Earth but of the universe itself.

Man can become the most magnificent creature in the universe if he can only break the habit of lifetimes by denying his own need for power, but in doing so, does not become complacent in his need to conserve, restrain and undo many of the iniquities that have evolved over lifetimes of habitual greed.

'Greed maketh man' is the current ideology. Ideology of the masses becomes the downfall of the few. No one who can manifest greed will ever be able to manifest truth, beauty and wisdom. Greed is the antithesis of how human beings were meant to live in the world.

Human beings were meant to understand who they are to the fullest extent possible, while greed reduces man's ability to feel himself as a partner in the world of which he is a part. No one can become wise if he is greedy, it is as simple as that. Greed is the manifest antithesis of wisdom.

Let us now come to the situation where man is able to regard all other men and other creatures in his world as equal.

*May we ask the reader to feel into the possibility that equality is possible on the planet for a moment. Feel yourself actually feeling equal to every other person on the planet, every other creature in the environment you live in.*

*Make a circle in your mind's eye and put the postman, the plumber, the toff, the mother, the child next door, the horse in the field, the rabbit over there, into your circle. Make a big, big circle and include more and more and more of the known and unknown people in your life into your circle.*

*What does that feel like? Is it comfortable enough for you to relax? Does it make you feel superior or inferior to have all these creatures in your circle? What do you want to do in the circle now all these people are included in your imagination as equals?*

*Does it feel better because you have always felt unequal to certain people or worse because the thought of some creature or person in your circle being equal to you is insupportable? Be honest, what does equality feel like right now? Pretty difficult we imagine.*

Equality has been possible in several eras in the ancient past. The most successful was in China in the early years of recorded history. Many aspects of the feudal system were able to allow all people the dignity of being what and who they were in the environment. Many feudal barons were able to allow their worker farmers to reach a measure of independence that allowed them to become aware of their own important value to the whole system.

The Cathars, the heretical sect in twelfth century France, enabled the masses to reach a level of dignity that ennobled their aim to manifest Godliness in their everyday lives, even though the Parfait, the hierarchical sect of perfected ones, made this more difficult, as the value system of equality became tainted with spiritual greed in the end.

Manifest greed became the way of life in eighteenth century Britain because the Industrial Revolution made the manufacturing of goods the goal of human endeavour in a way that has never been seen on the planet before. Industrial espionage, industrial spying, became the fuel in which the race for more and more and more goods became the way of life in modern times.

Make the leap of faith that greed is the result of more and more goods and services being emptied on to the market place. We suggest the most important aspect of becoming happy with life in the present moment will be to establish the relationship between what you need, and what you think you need, to become a well-rounded human being.

Desire for more is the most insidious aspect of human nature today, and desire for wisdom one of the least desired aspects of humanity. If humanity truly desired wisdom it would understand that greed for goods is not the way to happiness – ever.

May we suggest the way to wisdom is to let go the need for desire by really looking at the motivation of such desire. Desire is a drive to combat loneliness. Loneliness is the basic human condition in that we all arrive on the planet alone and we all die alone. In between, we believe we need to shore up that intrinsic loneliness with gifts to ourselves and others that will fill a wide gaping hole, a well of loneliness, and fear that we are unsafe on the planet we live on.

May we suggest the way to happiness is to understand loneliness in a deeper way and to respect that loneliness in ourselves, as the motivational force to wisdom.

Wisdom is understanding the basic nature of our humanness.

Loneliness is the misunderstanding that we are alone on the planet, because loneliness is manifestly what we feel.

*Now make an effort to reduce your breath to a minimum for a moment. Make the breathing very very shallow inside the lungs and ask yourself what this shallow breathing makes you feel. Can you sense a very very lonely person inside that shallow breathing? Can you make the leap of faith that this is what you are feeling?*

*Make the breathing even more shallow and feel the person who feels lonely feeling very, very afraid of such aloneness. Can you feel that fear? Now let that fear circulate around the body in such a way that you really do want to hide away from everyone because you cannot make the effort to communicate that fear to anyone. Let the fear feel very very bad until a small creature that is you begins to worry that he may never feel safe again on the planet.*

*Now drop that feeling. Just drop it and begin to take deep breaths again, deep deep breaths into the lungs where the air feels warm and moisty and circulating beautifully around the body.*

*Feel the difference in how you feel. Feel the wonderful sense of aliveness that comes suddenly because you are breathing boldly and fully, taking into your lungs the wonderful air that is available to everyone on the planet to breathe fully into the human world of men and women. How does that make you feel? Does it make you feel very, very safe suddenly? Safer than you have felt for years? Does it?*

We suggest that in fact the reason most human beings feel so unsafe on the planet is that they have never ever breathed properly. They have come onto the planet in such a state of fear of loneliness that they have forgotten how to breathe properly. Breath is the breath of life, and if people cannot breathe in life they are afraid that life cannot support them safely. Remember that. To breathe is to live life; and to live life in a sense of safety, we need to breathe in life deeply, wisely and magnificently.

Many people are afraid to feel safe in case they make mistakes in life. Life is one big learning ground and the way to regard life is to really accept that there will be mistakes and that mistakes are meant to be made. That's what makes us learn about life. Our mistakes are the fuel by which we move forward into the next phase of our life.

On the other hand there are no mistakes because we are motivated to move forward by mistakes that are the result of our moving forward. We create our mistakes in order to move forward! Does that make sense?

May we suggest that in the past, mistakes were regarded as dumb things to do and punished by jumping down our own throats, or other people's throats. Blame leads to shame, and shame is again one of the most fundamental aspects of human existence right now. Shame makes people feel unsafe again, but shame is not the most critical way to beat ourselves up. That accolade goes to the most influential aspect of negative thinking in ourselves, money.

Money was instituted in order to exchange goods and services. It was literally a convenience that occurred, so that more and more goods and services could be devised for sharing. Before that people were limited in their ability to make things to share and bargain for, and man was therefore limited in his constant desire for more and more and more.

Money has become a God of the first order, hasn't it? Money has become the bargaining tool that creates the hierarchical system we have spoken of. It has taken the place of God in many instances because God does not seem to be able to give man more and more and more in the way money can. Money, then, is the way we expect ourselves to be judged by. Not only judged by the person next door, but also by ourselves.

If we don't have money we are unworthy to be considered a reasonable human being. Money maketh man. No one remembers any longer that goods and services are about ease of living a wise, dedicated life, of natural rhythm and beauty; a way to express the innate creativity that resides in man, that needs to be expressed if he is to feel valued as a valuable human being.

The production of the goods or services is no longer valid for its own sake, but simply as a means to find more value in the God of money itself. Money, money money, it's the rich man world.

Or is it? Or is it? Let's be serious here. Is money able to bring happiness? True happiness? If anyone says yes then they simply don't have any idea of the true way that man is meant to live on the planet.

Man is meant to be a representative, a representative of the inner dynamic of the whole universe, by which we mean the inner realms of space which are able to be manifested inside the human being himself in order to resonate with and understand the working of the universe.

A tall order? You've got to believe it because until human beings accept that they are responsible for the way in which the universe is able to evolve, the universe will not be able to move forward in the way it needs, to sustain life in the myriad dimensions it has done so far.

May we suggest the maxim 'as above, so below' makes the reality of the human condition very clear. The human being is capable of resonating inside to the whole universal mechanism, and as such can manifest the necessary energy to sustain life on Earth and on every planet in the firmament – though in a very different way to that which manifests on Earth. Quite a task ahead, we suggest.

More and more people are beginning to experience the stirrings of discontent with the status quo, aren't they? More and more people are opting for simpler lifestyles; down-sizing as it's called. By doing so they are releasing themselves from the most insidious aspect of human conditioning, greed. And in this way they are opening themselves up to the possibility of understanding the way Nature works and the way the human being as part of Nature, has the incredible opportunity to manifest all that is, inside his being. All that is, no more no less.

The human being, once he has let go the desire to know more, grow more, and buy more, will naturally begin to allow his own relationship to life to become more tranquil, more manifestly decent and ultimately more in touch with the truth of human nature. Again we repeat, when man has lost his desire for more he will understand it all. And we mean, ALL.

So, to recap. We want the reader to make a leap of faith that he can find happiness in exactly the way he is now, without exception. Happiness has nothing to do with how much he earns, or where he lives, or how he makes his living. It is to do with living in a state of grace in the present moment, without anything or anyone making him wish he was somewhere else.

Making a commitment to happiness means letting go the need to become something we are not, but at the same time making a total commitment to becoming fully who we are.

*Now feel the way you feel at hearing this. Sceptical, excited, resistant, happy? Allow whatever feeling is taking place to really resonate all over the body. Feel the way it feels, where in the body do you feel it most this feeling? Make a decision to concentrate on that part of the body now and accentuate the way you feel to a very high degree. Let the body speak to you about what you feel in this regard. Happy, sceptical, mean, resentful? Let it become very very uncomfortable in that feeling, unless you are feeling happy!*

*Now drop the feeling completely, let it go. Make a decision to believe the possibility that indeed you can be happy exactly how you are, without exception. Make a decision that the idea of making something of your life, other than worrying that you are feeling fed up because you haven't got enough money or enough information or enough love or enough matchsticks, can become a search for happiness in a very new way.*

*Make the decision today that for the next twenty, forty, sixty years of your life you will make a real effort to understand that life isn't at all the way you were led to believe it was. Then make the decision to continue reading the book so that bit by bit, sentence by sentence, something can begin to happen inside yourself that will be totally convincing.*

Experiencing life is not such a difficult thing to be convinced about, is it? Experiencing the way the stars shine in the firmament, experiencing the way the flowers feel at the end of the day, experiencing the most incredible inner peace cannot be difficult when the idea is so appealing, can it?

Make space in your life for the little things in life to become the basis of much that is unintelligible to you. Accept the inevitable that the time will come when no one will be able to succeed at the expense of others and of the planet itself. That day is coming sooner than anyone can imagine.

Make sure you are a person who makes sure the world is intelligible to you by realising that inside you is the whole universe, if only you would believe it and desire it. Making the commitment to understand yourself is the way to understand all that is. That is the way human beings are made and the way human destiny is evolving. It's quite an adventure, isn't it?

Let the adventure become a true spiritual quest because it is the spiritual nature of man that unlocks the universe to his immortal Soul being. That is the meaning of the Soul; a mediator between Heaven and Earth that allows all people, whatever race, creed, colour, gender or persuasion, to understand the true meaning of the universe and the part the human being plays in the unfolding drama of Life itself.

Scientists have been able to resist the fact that the world has a spiritual dimension, not just a material one. May we suggest the way forward to a happy, simple, peaceful and magnificent life is truly to accept who you are, what you are, and how you are in this life, knowing that at another time, another place, your soul has incarnated into life in a myriad different disguises to reveal to you the truth of the universe. Life is far far more complex and far far simpler than anyone can ever imagine it to be.

Start now and take a journey to the meaning and understanding that is inherent in man and the universe. Make it a fun journey, but also a serious one. Man is a magnificent being in the universe. Earth is the learning zone for such magnificence.

It is a privilege to become a man on Earth and to experience the myriad meanings of life here. Take a look around you and trust that 'all shall be well and all manner of things shall be well'. Then be prepared to let go all the old value systems you have been committed to and just commit yourself to Life everlasting.

Can you?

# Chapter Two

## *MAKING SURE THE LIFE IS VIABLE*

We feel the way forward is to make sure the life you are leading is absolutely the best you can do under the circumstances in which you are now living. For example is the way you clean your teeth the best you are able to manage, given the amount of toothpaste you have and the number of minutes you have to do the job in the morning?

Or, do you need to take a few more minutes and dental floss your teeth? Or take a little longer to brush them up and down a few more times? In which case do you need to get up earlier to do so?

See what we mean? Everything you do needs to be appraised in the light of really understanding that life can be improved simply by seeing the best in every situation possible. Does that make sense?

In our view the real problem with people who are discontented with their lives is that they don't look hard enough at the things they do. They skirt over them in an attempt to move on to the more interesting things they think they <u>ought</u> to be doing. Remember the only thing of importance in life is doing what you are doing <u>right now</u> to the best of your ability – including cleaning your teeth!

May we ask our readers whether or not they think about cleaning their teeth when they are cleaning their teeth? We imagine not very many of you actually think about what you are doing. Very few in fact, isn't it?

May we offer some advice here on making sure the life is viable?

Think when you clean your teeth, but think about what you are doing to make your teeth the very best possible teeth you can make for yourself. Not about the dog who needs walking or the office cleaner who isn't doing his or her job properly.

May we offer another piece of advice? Don't forget to clean the toothbrush properly when you have finished, screw the top back on the toothpaste properly and clean the basin. All acts to make that part of your life absolutely the best you possibly can for yourself. Try it. It makes life seem much richer all of a sudden, we promise.

Now, down to the more meaningful things of life. May we offer yet more advice? Don't go without breakfast. Breakfast is the meal of the day when all the molecules begin to waken up again after the night's shut-down.

All right, chips and beans aren't exactly the best things for breakfast, but to be honest these are better than nothing. If you are going to do the absolute best for yourself then cold milk on cereal is ideal to keep the breath healthy and the molecules dancing.

What is important though is to really enjoy the breakfast you choose. That above all keeps the breath in good shape plus enjoyment of what we do – even if it is beans and chips! Enjoyment neutralises many of the odours that molecules dish up as they make themselves felt at the microbial level each morning. Microbes send out odours that need to be neutralised if we are to have fresh breath each morning.

Why fresh breath? Our breath is the means by which we greet the day and respond to the world at large. Breath is our mediating point with the Sun and it is the Sun which makes us feel at peace with the world each day – whether we can see it or not.

Breath is the sole means by which we make our relationship to the rest of the universe, let alone to our life force on this Earth. May we suggest to our readers that in the lifetime of the planet each human being's breath accounts for most of the universe's ability to sustain life in whatever form that might take.

Not the sort of life the scientists dream of, but the vaporised life that much of the life within the universe is made up of. Dimensional realities are sustained by the breath of Earth beings. Think about it.

Imagine an electron rushing forth, from its nucleus, towards another more positive polarity. The electron, though minuscule in proportion, makes a difference both to the nucleus and its intended target, just as the breath affects unseen dimensions. And the cumulative effect of millions of individual electrons keeps our world supplied by power. Does that make you wish to breathe more fully, more efficiently and more creatively than you imagined you could?

Here is an exercise to help you breathe more efficiently.

*Make a small dent in the middle of your back by standing upright and just a little backwards. Your stomach will stick out quite a bit if you make the dent properly. Now create a circulation of air by breathing into the chest and allowing the chest to rise upwards – that's the only way it will go easily if your stomach is extended. Then blow out the air through your mouth quite sharply but slowly, making your stomach stick out even more.*

*As your stomach distends, allow the base of your body to relax and letting go the posture allow the base of the body to move in a releasing, relaxing and circulatory manner.*

*Push out parts of the body to stretch out the tension in the sacral area (around the navel) which we suggest is notoriously under used, despite the predilection to believe the world is a sexually free and propitious place to be. If only you knew how tense, strained and under used the average sacral area is. But more of that in a later chapter.*

*Now, when all the tension feels released and the lower part of the body feels looser, stand up straight and breathe in a deep breath all the way down and into the sacral region. Get the sacral region more and more free by breathing in and then out, deep deep breaths that fill the whole body with wonderful tension releasing breaths of pure gold air.*

The body needs airing, believe us. No one on the planet really breathes in the full way the universe would have us do to release the dimensional aspects of human existence. If every human being were able to breathe in the full unhindered way it was meant to do, life in the universe would be beyond imagining – and available to many more eyes than it is already.

Imagine being in touch with the multi-dimensional universe you live in, simply by clearing away all the garbage that is trapped in the tense and materially based human body at this time by breathing more fully.

Now, may we ask the reader truthfully to explain in two sentences why their life at this moment doesn't feel as full as it ought to do? What is the problem you feel you face that doesn't make life quite right? May we suggest the way to answer this is to take yesterday as a prime example and write down why yesterday wasn't really as good as you wanted it to be.

Perhaps the main reason yesterday wasn't brilliant was because the partner in your life wasn't able to meet your needs, or perhaps the reason is that if you hadn't had to do something for someone else – like your boss – you might have done something better for your own amusement? Or even that you have so much money you couldn't really decide which piece of property to buy next?

Well, write it down in two sentences exactly what the problem was about yesterday. Can you do that? In two sentences? No, of course not. It would take at least three pages to explain fully what was really wrong with yesterday, if you took the time to look deeply into the issue of how to make your life viable at this moment.

Let us see how to make life viable in myriad different ways now, so that the next few years can become a very different sort of life into the millennium. In several years time the Earth will be a very different place to the one it is now.

Make sure you don't miss out on the adventure of a lifetime, by regretting so much of the life you have now. The secret to making the next few years anxiety and pain free is to let yourself really know how to live life to the fullest possible degree. Here are a few clues to this seemingly impossible task.

Make sure the garden is up to date. What do we mean by that? Feel the way you feel about your garden right now. Is it feeling a drag on the resources? A drag on your mind because it never gets done until the last minute, and then you have to scourge the garden for being such a messy patch of ground in your busy life?

What is the extent to which you feel the garden is a bit of a nuisance to be coped with whenever you have a spare minute and even then something else crops up to annoy you because it was meant to be the one time you could do the garden?

Feel the way you want to do things but never seem to do them and then on the one day you do want to do it, something else takes priority. What happens? You actually set inside yourself a level of tension that creates a circuit of anxiety, to add to other circuits of anxiety, that have set themselves in train at other times this 'should/shouldn't' push-pull situation has come into existence.

That is a lot of tension, isn't it? Now, the way to stop this band of tension is to make sure you do the garden, or the garage clearing, or even go to the theatre, at exactly the time you both want to do it and can do it. Does that make sense?

All you need do is to decide what needs doing and make a list. Then take a deep breath and decide which of those things you actually <u>want</u> to do right now. <u>Want to do right now</u>. Not what you ought to do, what you can't be bothered to do, what you feel is driving you crazy because it should have been done last week.

No, find out the thing on your list that you actually want to do right now. There will be one of those things that amazingly is at exactly the right time to do that task. It will feel possible suddenly to do that thing, NOW. In the NOW.

Are we making ourselves clear here? Whatever you do in your life, it needs to be very clear that the NOW of your life is actually what you want to be doing in your life, NOW.

In most cases the reason why something feels too boring to be done now is that there is never enough time to do all things there are to do. Or so it seems. But in fact there is always time to do everything there is to do, if the thing you do now is what you want to do.

No more tension in the being, is there, if you start really enjoying everything you do NOW? Now is actually an endless moment of time, if you really learn to live in the Now time of livingness.

Now holds all there is in the universe, because Now is the only moment that is connected to the space time continuum – that ever was, ever is and ever will be, world without end. To live in the Now of human existence is the only goal of the human being that will lead him to a real understanding of life everlasting.

It may feel easy to live in the now but believe us it is the hardest thing for the average human being to accomplish because either he lives in the past or he lives in the future. Never, ever in the NOW.

Begin to learn to live in the Now by recognising that Now is the hour for all good children to come to the aid of humanity by learning to look for what you can do in the Now and enjoy that Now moment beyond measure.

To do NOW, what you want to do now, allows the length of time it takes to do 'that Now thing' to diminish. Without straining at something, there is an ease of production that makes the task such a pleasure that it can be done in no time at all.

Writing a book at the precise moment at which it is 'meant' to be written, allows the words to flow in such a manner that all the days of anxiety when it was not possible to write the book are forgotten.

How much better not to have had those days of punishment – which set up those bands of anxiety we spoke about earlier – and simply to have waited until the Now moment presented itself. Far less hazardous on the body and far quicker in the long run to do it when it 'wanted' to be done. That applies to all things, at all times. The NOW moment is sacrosanct.

This is a kind of Feng Shui of life, isn't it? Feng Shui in Chinese heritage is a means of saying that all things have a right place at a right time in space and time. Man is the only creature in the universe who has to battle with time and space in quite this way.

But the rule of the universe, other than for man, is that matter needs to be organised in such a way that it has a 'rightness' about it, an intrinsic sense of the place it needs to be in order for it to have meaning in the universe.

Man cannot see that if a tree or plant or house is not placed in line with its intrinsic rightness of place or position, then the energy surrounding that tree or plant or house will not be conducive to receiving the most propitious influences. Like the human body it will create a level of tension in its energy field which no one will feel comfortable in.

Man has 'forgotten' the sensitivity to place and spirit that he was born with millennia ago. It is time to retrieve the art that China brought back into its memory from time immemorial and understand that in the world of man there is a moment in time in which something in space is most advantageously presented.

In our view what needs to be experienced again is the way in which trees and plants and animals do have a level of consciousness that man understands inside himself, but has forgotten.

What man can experience in himself needs to be understood by making a leap of faith that in the coming centuries man will be making enormous strides in the consciousness of how the Earth herself is making herself felt in the consciousness of human beings now. And in turn how the consciousness of man is getting in touch with aspects of the universe that scientists would wonder at, if they could believe with their hearts and not with their eyes, what is now happening to mankind on Earth.

May we suggest the most valuable way to remember the time when all men were able to understand their relationship to the trees and plants and animals might be to do this exercise.

*Take a few minutes to settle down into your seat. Make sure the balls of your feet are on the ground because the most important part of the exercise is to really feel a connection to the living Earth beneath your feet. Are you sitting comfortably? Then let us begin.*

*Feel a new sense of peace at the base of your body now that you have shaken it out of its lethargy and tension. Feel a real feeling of happiness in the base of your body, because the base of your body is the way you contact the trees and the grass and the matter of things in your being.*

*Feel the grass beneath your feet in your imagination. Feel the swathes of beautiful green grass below you now, and imagine a small pond nearby. Take a long cool breath of air into your lungs and feel a breeze on your face, as though a breath of air has started to blow around you in a lazy, hazy summer's day mood.*

*Now look over at the pond and <u>feel</u> a frog in the pond. Don't think about it, just feel it in the pond, swimming around that pond on this hazy day of summer, ready to poke its head up out of the water so you, on your patch of grass, can see its head just surfacing the water now.*

*Feel your relationship to that frog suddenly. Feel a sense of getting to know that frog face when you look at its head poking out of the water – at the same time <u>feel</u> the way frog feels as it comes up out of the water and looks at you. You <u>can</u> feel a simultaneous sense of being frog and being you – it is possible, you know. Lift your head up a bit as though you are frog poking its head out of the water and <u>feel</u> how frog feels right now.*

*So, how does frog feel? Can he see you or feel you watching him watching you? No, he can't, can he? He isn't aware of you in any particular way at all. Not like you are aware of him is he?*

*Let frog feel what frog feels and feel what you feel. Does it feel the same? Not at all. Frog feels more whole, somehow. In touch with his beingness so that what he sees is just part of being and doing together. You are just part of his environment, aren't you? Not <u>you</u>, as frog is frog to you. See what we mean?*

*Now look up and see the willow tree over the pond. Can you imagine a willow tree, whatever size you feel appropriate for your particular pond and feel willow overhanging your pond now? Feel willow now inside the base of your body. Feel a sense of willowness inside now.*

*Don't think, just trust that your intention to feel willow creates willow inside your being. Feel willow and tell us what willow tells you about frog. Is frog all right in his pond, right now? Does he want for anything in his pond? Is he waiting for food, or resting in the pond while the sun filters through the willow on to his resting body?*

Make the choice now. Do you believe you can be in touch with Nature and understand what Nature is thinking and feeling, or are you prepared to go on in ignorance of the incredible interaction that happens in Nature between Nature and around Nature?

One day ecologists will ask Nature herself what her problems are, not assume to know it all, by taking for granted that man has wrecked the planet willy nilly for his own purposes – which of course he has, and it needs to be rectified.

But that is not the whole story. Man was part of an enormous plan that evolution has been carrying out almost imperceptibly over millions and millions of years. Man has piecemeal destroyed the Earth over the last two hundred decades certainly, but there is a plan in which the Earth is party to its own demise in the form that has been evolving over these millennia.

Part of the plan has been to raise the consciousness of planet Earth by releasing it from a lower strain of energetic resonance. Part of the plan has been for man to raise his consciousness to match the incoming energetic frequencies from universal sources so that the Earth herself can reconstitute at a higher frequency.

So, you can see that ecology is a crude response to what is a far far bigger change in the vibration of the Earth's atmosphere to withstand the incoming changes universe-wide. Evolution is not Darwinian. It is, if anything, Einsteinian. And more. Much, much, more.

So much to learn, isn't there? And the brain is not the mechanism with which to learn it. The imagination is. Imagine! Life is lived through imagination, not thinking. Quite confronting for scientists and ecologists alike.

Now let's get back to making sure the life is viable at the micro level. This life. Your life. Now. What is more, this is the only way to truly understand how to live life at the macro level of understanding that we speak of. Simplicity can unfold into the greatest level of diversity mankind has ever experienced consciously.

Down-sizing is the route to making sure you are in the running for the most incredible renaissance in human history that is about to hit planet Earth.

Why down-sizing? May we suggest that instead of basing everything anyone ever thinks about on money, there is a moment when it occurs to almost everyone that money does not, and never will, create a lifestyle of contentment.

May we ask the reader to deny that? Even if you won the lottery we guarantee that within a few weeks, unless you are one of the very very few people who doesn't reflect at least occasionally on what they are doing in their life, you will feel deflated. There will be a feeling of 'so what' about that million pounds, even if it takes a while, because you are too busy spending it to notice the deflation. May we ask anyone to defy us on that?

Most people in the West, who on the whole have plenty, rub along through life. They don't, if they are honest, feel they are in touch with life in the way that deep down they know they yearn for. To be in touch with life is to stop thinking about money. It's as simple as that. Once anyone stops thinking about money they will be able to settle into a pattern of relationship to life that will lead them towards a more satisfying relationship to all there is.

And believe us there is so much more than anyone ever dreams of.

Once money is out of the equation there will be a vast whole to be explored, won't there? Think about it in this way. Most people are busy earning a living. Of course that is absolutely necessary to become what most people think they want to become. Successful. But what is success?

Success to most people is to be seen to be successful. To uphold a position which, in themselves, they feel is necessary to be someone in the eyes of someone else. However big or small the earning the need is the same, to be identified with a persona that says 'this is the me I want people to think is me'.

But if it is based on money, as we have said before, it is based on power over. Not potency to create a better image of oneself. An image that tells the truth about who one is. May we suggest that in truth who one is, is absolutely nothing to do with anything that most people think it is and absolutely nothing to do with how much money we have at any one time.

In fact, we guarantee that most unhappiness comes to people who have inherited vast sums of money from family property, and never ever feel they have earned the right to that money. Earning a right to money is simply another way of suppressing a gaping hole inside the being which cannot be filled any other way at this moment. Having vast sums of unearned money simply keeps the gaping hole wider open and more obvious.

What does it mean to earn a living? Who says one man is worth more than another person in this climate of valuing a man for the job he does, not for his intrinsic value as a human being? The hierarchical system values men (and now women to a certain extent) by judging what is valuable, and what is not valuable, in human society.

May we suggest that in the not too distant future, value will take an unexpected and sudden turn, and leave many people who continue to judge on this outmoded basis flailing in the breeze.

So to make it more clear, we suggest that down-sizing is a continuing trend, as more and more people realise that money has not given them what they wanted. Indeed that money has clouded their ability to realise that life is a precious commodity that no one has really taken seriously, because they have been earning money so earnestly.

May we suggest that fear of that gaping hole will reveal many people in the future who are unable to take life by the hands and really understand that the world they are living in is changed and changing at a pace that most people would be terrified of, if they could see what is happening in the ethers now.

But, if people do continue to hang on to the God of money they will miss the boat, it's as simple as that. Find a way of becoming realistic about the money you have now and don't allow yourself to hanker after more and more money. Hanker after Life now.

Hanker after an understanding of the real value of other people now, especially those who, in your race to have more money, you have tried to ignore. Homelessness, New Age travellers, money losses at Lloyds, are all indications that the system is changing and that local authorities in particular will have to re-evaluate what is important in 'Life' as opposed to 'the Economy'.

We offer an exercise to look at money in a new way.

*Allow yourself to feel very very rich suddenly. Imagine yourself feeling like a potentate in some foreign country. Millions of dollars are yours at the touch of a button. Touch the button now and feel so rich you cannot imagine anything on the planet that you cannot buy with your money right now.*

*What would you buy first? Feel how it feels to be able to buy anything you want in the world right now. What would you buy with that money? The first thing? A watch? A boat? A homestead?*

*Feel each thing in your body as you decide to buy the things you've always wanted. A watch? Yes, well. Why not a watch? A boat? Feel into your solar plexus right now and put a boat inside the solar plexus. What does it make you feel? A boat to sail across the seas – with a crew of course to do your bidding. Yes? Does that feel possible?*

*Perhaps. Another house perhaps? And another? And another? Put each purchase into the solar plexus and feel what you really feel about purchasing more and more and more items.*

*Feel how quickly, if you allow yourself to truly feel inside the solar plexus, how boring it is to buy yet more 'stuff'. Feel it deeply, this boredom with buying things. Because believe us, it does become boring to always buy, never to experience life. And boredom is a sign that there is a gaping hole in life that cannot ever be filled with buying things, only by experiencing life to its fullest extent at any one time.*

*Now let go the potentate – if you can spare the time from choosing yet more 'things' to clutter your life! And put inside your solar plexus a homeless person. Someone who has felt let down by life or love, or by the powers that be, and is left to beg on the streets. Don't think about this person as you might normally think of them, but put that person in your solar plexus right now. What happens?*

*What do you get in your solar plexus? Fear? Happiness? Love? What do you feel about this person in your solar plexus? Let's look at the circumstances of your life.*

*There but for the Grace of God go I, and depending on your inner relationship to fear of that fact you may feel compassionate or fearful. One or the other we suggest. Compassion or Fear.*

Compassion is the very highest form of love. It is not sentimental, emotional love, it is compassion – a far more detached relationship to the feelings inside your body, and in our view a far more realistic way to respond to situations that arise in life where either fear or love are the main feelings a human being has.

A human being who attains compassion – like Christ perhaps – is able to adjust to the inequities of life with a keener eye than those whose sentiment oozes out all over the place, allowing themselves to wallow in situations that come their way – to make their own lives more palatable we suggest.

Today's task, to make life more viable is to let go fear and to realign to compassion. No mean task is it, but in doing so we promise there will be such an outpouring of compassion that there will be a totally new relationship to the whole of life and its searing inconsistencies. Once fear is let go, and human beings establish compassion as their motivating force, life becomes viable in the most astonishing ways.

To sum up: Life becomes viable when we live in the Now, when we learn to communicate with the whole of life – and that means the natural world as well as the multi-dimensional world. But above all, life becomes viable when we let go our possession and obsession with money, which allows us to let go fear and realign to compassion. Are you game?

# Chapter Three

# *RELEASING EVERYTHING THAT ISN'T YOU*

May we suggest the most important thing to remember these days is to hold on to your hat! By which we mean, hold on to the thing that makes you uniquely who you are. Wearing a hat makes someone stand out amongst the crowd who are not wearing hats; and in our view what needs to be achieved by every single human being on the planet is their own uniqueness.

Simple as it sounds, it is the most underrated and ignored theme in peoples lives today. Uniqueness is utterly ignored by most people because the need to conform to a stereotype has taken over the identities of every individual on the planet – even those cultures that are allowed to express their uniqueness don't, or rather cannot do so, because they have no idea where to look for that unique being who is there.

May we show you how this came into being – that no one remembers who they are any more – by relating a story of the Garden of Eden? When God decided to release his image on the world of man He made up his mind to allow two kinds of creatures to inhabit the Earth.

One was a man creature who made up the bulk of the inhabitants of Earth, the other was a Sun creature who decided to mate with Earth men in order to divulge the nature of the universe and God to Earth beings in due time, when the time was suitable for the Earth to understand its true nature.

The Sun beings were sent to Earth to mate with Earth beings in the way that mating was staged in those days – asexually. Man had the potential to know that he was a divine being made in the image of God, provided he was in touch with that part of himself that knew he was a God man and not only an Earth man.

Unfortunately, as in all human experience, a sacrifice was made by the Sun beings. In deciding to mate with the earthlings, Sun beings felt an enormous ache for their Sun beingness; their purest Sun beingness, which had to be overshadowed to a great degree by earthliness for a very long time before man became conscious enough to recognise the divine part of his nature.

In that ache was a wound that never ever felt ameliorated throughout the history of time from then on. These wounds to the Sun being – and therefore incorporated into the human experience at all times – were categorised into five themes: Betrayal, Denial, Rejection, Abandonment and Abuse. Even though they agreed to do this marvellous work for Earth beings they looked on it as a betrayal, or denial, or rejection, or abandonment, or abuse by God.

Within every human being is an innate feeling that they have been 'let down by God', to the extent that everyone on the planet carries a wound of such moment that until now this wound has acted as the sole motivating force within each individual human being on the planet. No one on Earth is without a wound, experienced as one or other of the wounds above and often feeling like an overdose of all five.

Look back at your life and feel whether or not you could say, if you are totally honest, that you haven't felt one or other of these wounds conducting your life. No one, we suggest, is capable of living life as it is conducted right now without feeling wounded and, if you are honest again, without making your whole life a sort of barrier against such a wound. We feel an exercise would help to establish whether or not this is so for you.

*Exercise 1 on tape*

*Make yourself comfortable in the seat as best you can. Now let the mind go completely. Let the mind drop down through your body and out through your feet. Feel the anxieties drop down through the body and out into the ground through your feet.*

*Don't worry if you still feel a little anxious, but do your best to relax. Feel as comfortable as you can. Relax as best you can and now instead of feeling tense, <u>allow</u> a feeling of tension to build up around the solar plexus.*

*Feel the tension building up in the solar plexus and describe it to yourself. Is it a sick feeling or a discomforting feeling? Describe it to yourself in as critical detail as possible. Don't spare yourself, let the feeling build up and up until it really says something to you about discomfort and unhappiness.*

*Don't worry that it won't go away again. This is a safe exercise and one that we often do with clients. If it becomes unbearable all you need do is break the circuit by taking a deep breath and expiring the feelings out through the feet into the Earth and open your eyes.*

*So you have this uncomfortable feeling in your solar plexus. Allow it to build and build and then put your mother into the solar plexus. Place a picture of your mother, if you can, on top of this feeling of sickness, discomfort, however you have described it to yourself. Feel the feeling the mother engenders in you at this moment in time.*

*Don't think, don't allow any known feelings to take over, just allow a picture of your mother into these sick feelings in your solar plexus. Now, put next to your mother an image of you at the age of three.*

*Not a picture you know but an imaginary sense of yourself at three years old, maybe younger, maybe older, but set the intention of becoming three years old, with your mother beside you, as you are feeling the awful discomfort you have described.*

*Now feel the feelings of this scenario. <u>Feel</u> them, don't <u>think</u> about it. Just feel the feelings inside yourself, and tell yourself what that basic feeling is. What does that feeling tell you about your wound? What is the wound you are feeling when you are in this situation with your mother at three – or thereabouts?*

**Rejection? Denial? Betrayal? Abandonment? Abuse?**

*You'll be surprised how much a feeling comes to be described in one way or another by one of these wounds – or all five of them – but dig deeply to discover which of these wounds is your major de-energiser and feel it deeply.*

*Now feel that wound and tell yourself quickly what you have done all your life to keep that wound at bay. What have you done to barrier yourself from this gaping heartache of a wound?*

*Maybe you have staged a rebellion since the age of three. Perhaps you have coined a phrase like 'damn you, I'm off'? Or made sure you don't ever get caught by a demon that's chasing you? Maybe you have decided to 'show you', that the world owes you a living for feeling so lousy?*

*Whatever, we want to suggest that the reason no one on the planet feels safe is that the most stable person in our lives, our mother, represents God to us in the early years of our lives and mother sets up the feeling of abandonment, rejection, abuse, betrayal or denial, simply by cutting the umbilical cord and letting us float freely in the world – like God did to his Sun beings.*

*Quite a revelation, don't you see? Mother is, by her very nature, our bugbear in this life. She sets up a whole memory bank of feeling wounded that neither she, nor you, can do anything about, until now.*

*Because it's time to let go this wound once and for all, isn't it? It's time to feel absolutely free from reacting against a wound that is set in the genetic structure of our invisible beings. Until we get rid of our wound we will never ever be free to become fully who we are and respond naturally to the world as a human being who is both material and divine; and whose journey on Earth throughout history has been to discover the extent of that divinity and how it magnifies us to the Lord, as it were.*

*Do make sure that the feelings engendered by the exercise are now totally gone from your being. Let them go. Breathe deeply and coolly into the solar plexus and allow the feelings to dissipate, right now. Don't worry if they hang around for a while, this is a very powerful exercise and may come as a shock to experience. Allow yourself to absorb the information in a quiet manner and then let the feelings disappear of their own volition.*

Mother is not to blame for your misgivings about life necessarily, but she is the perpetrator of an age-old manifestation of woundedness. Your life story is your life story, but the wound you carry is everyman's woundedness. It was the sacrifice made by the Sun beings in the universe, who made man the magnificent creature he is capable of becoming in due time.

Don't let mother take the blame any more for your misgivings. Make a determined effort to accept the consequences of being a human being on this Earth now and allow a new atmosphere to penetrate the being from now on.

May we suggest the next release that needs to be made is the misconception that man is the centre of the universe. He isn't. But he is the most important material creature in the universe in the sense that the Earth is a totally significant place to be right now.

In our view what man needs, before he can become who he truly is meant to be, is to become aware of the most important aspect of his nature; his divine Soul, which means letting go the sense that he is the centre of the universe. May we show you what we mean?

In the beginning of time man was created in God's image. That means he was made to become the evolutionary human being he is today, but with a growing awareness that he is to become the God within himself, not to continue to worship the God outside the framework of his own experience.

In our view each human being needs to remember something of his past history in order to understand that moment by moment he is letting go his experience of God, in order to replace it with an evolutionary understanding of the universal framework in which he is operating.

In other words, God keeps changing places in man's consciousness in order to release the unfolding process towards the ultimate realisation that God is in all things and that man is the measure of all things ultimately.

May we suggest that in the coming months there will be a magnificent shift in consciousness that will begin to gnaw away inside the beings who until now have been unable to sense the shifts away from the material dimensions into the understanding of the spiritual laws behind the material.

Many others, who have already begun the journey towards this understanding of their spiritual selves, will begin to feel the pull towards knowing a shift has taken place and begin to feel themselves as an intrinsic part of the destiny of the universe, in that they can become aware of their multi-dimensional selves in a very heightened manner.

Most individuals, as yet, are unable to resist the lure of the material dimension, creating an even greater fog around them than they could possibly imagine. The shock of their realisation therefore, will be even greater than for anyone who was able to clear their vision sooner.

We feel the most significant realisation will be that there is absolutely no safety in money and only safety in the 'lap of the Gods', as it were; in the knowing that one is, and always has been, part of a safe universe in which man is just one small cog of an ever-changing wheel.

It is the fact that the face of God is ever-changing that creates the feeling of insecurity, but if man can become aware of himself as the creator of that constantly changing face of God, then he, too, can become a constantly changing creature without feeling the world is collapsing around him.

May we show you what we mean by God's ever-changing face? It needs an acceptance that each Soul incarnates many many times throughout the journey towards self actualisation, self knowledge and the return to God's garden of Eden on Earth.

*May we suggest the reader takes a cushion and sits on the floor. Make sure the cushion is comfortable and that if necessary the back is supported against a chair or whatever feels safe to you.*

*Make the decision to really understand the changing nature of God in order to recognise the fear you have of change in your life, because it is the recognition of the fear of change that will enable you to risk change in whatever circumstances you find yourself; and not to sit rigid with fear in the face of changes that are now inevitable in your life.*

*Feel the floor with your hands now and make the decision to really let go anything that is stopping you experience the changing face of God and thus your ability to change in circumstances that demand a new view of yourself in the future.*

*Let the ground feel safe beneath you and let the breath come and go in a relaxed manner now. Let the breath come and go, come and go in a slow rhythmic fashion, in order to really feel in touch with yourself, the ground and the fact that you are safe in the seat on the floor.*

*Now let the breath become more shallow, let the breath begin to feel less easy now and feel the panic it creates in the heart, because having less breath brings a level of fear that makes you uneasy. To have less air makes you feel very very fearful, doesn't it? It's a fear of not having breath that creates a feeling of panic, yes?*

*Now allow the breath to lengthen, to really become a long, slow 'in and out' kind of breath, making the in-breath go right down inside the body and out, down into the Earth in a deep arc, returning to the body and up and out through the top of the head to the heavens and down and round on the in-breath.*

*Let the breath circulate warmly and slowly in this manner for several breaths, in order to begin to feel a warm, cosy, relaxed feeling in the world of men.*

So breath is important, and not to have breath feels very challenging indeed. Death then is challenging because it means the breath is absolutely ready to leave the body and most people on the planet are fearful that their breath will leave them and they will be dead. It's as simple as that. Breath is the difference between life and death. Death is non-breath, Life is breath.

Change is death. It requires endless, continuing deaths and no wonder we are afraid to die. But let us show you how to become aware that change is not death but new life in the making; in which the world changes atmospherically and becomes a new dawn in which life everlasting can become a new moment of everlasting life.

*Exercise 2 on tape*

*Make a circle around where you are sitting, in your imagination. You are absolutely safe in this circle and are in no danger of dying, only experiencing the death of God over the millennia, in which a new dawn is created moment by moment. May we show you what we mean?*

*Make the decision to really allow yourself to travel back in time, to the dawn of time now, and allow the feelings to be what they are, in whatever way they choose to be. Make a sign of the cross to acknowledge that God is involved in these images and create the safe space that you have been asked to do.*

*Now really understand that in the moment of change it feels like a small death, but remember that all death becomes life everlasting until the next small death. Create a sense of continuing, cyclical movement by really feeling the breath now, coursing up in really large swoops of movement in a long slow in-breath, down and out through the feet, and up and round the heavens and down and down and out and round.*

*Let the cyclical movement feel good and slow and really in touch with a rhythmic sense of life and death. Up and out, down and round, allowing the body to begin to sense a real moment of joy that there is a long, slow rhythmical sense of safety in the body now.*

*Let the body feel very heavy, but let the mind free float in some way that allows the being to feel really alive to the elemental particle state of being. Feel the wave motion in the breath and feel the feeling of being intensely alive in the mind now, by creating a marker point to look at in the mind's eye.*

*Let the marker point be something safe like a buoy on the sea or a feeling that makes you want to take part in an adventure, whatever makes you feel ready to see the death of God in a vibrant exciting manner.*

*Now, allow the mind's eye to really understand the way the being has understood God over the millennia and how that understanding of God has changed and is constantly changing. Really feel the sense that there is now a feeling of change in the experience, by making the decision to do so, right now.*

*Feel a sort of machine in the mind's eye that will begin to reveal the sort of information you need to have right now. A visual scenario of the changing face of God.*

*We feel you will feel in the mind's eye a sense of making the decision to feel God as a man of judgement. He is a man of judgement who feels ready to judge you now at the Court of Judgement Day. He feels like a worthy man. He is a just man, but He judges man, doesn't He?*

*Is He in his judgement robes? What does He make you feel? Does He make you feel very small, totally insignificant as you come before Him in the Court of Judgement Day? Does God feel very large and overpowering?*

*How does He make you feel? Sense the feeling of God's judgement over you and tell yourself how you feel about it. What is He making you do on the Day of Judgement? Is He suggesting you look at your life again and find the places where you didn't live up to your own expectations?*

*Is He making you feel sorry for your peccadilloes, your inability to make the grade in some way? Do you feel you are being weighed up? What is the feeling you feel when you look at your past deeds and are made to feel very very ashamed?*

*What is He making you do, somehow? Is He making you live your life aright? Sentence is handed down, of penance for past sins and an expectation of you to create a new balance. Bringing balance to the life, isn't it? It's an external judgement on your life, isn't it?*

*Now, let that go, and feel a different God in the mind's eye. Feel a merry mountain of Godness, so to speak. A mountain that holds the Gods that tell man how to behave, moment by moment.*

*Can you sense a mountain of Gods and Goddesses who tell man how he is to behave in the world? Can you feel the idea of principles, of laying down archetypal behaviour for man to adhere to? In what way did they order man in this universal relationship to life? Could they provide a framework of order and guidelines, a sort of user's manual?*

*And what happened if man couldn't do it right, what happened? What did the Gods say, or do? Is there a feeling that the Gods and Goddesses themselves will energetically re-balance you? A sense that your life and times are totally in their hands?*

*Now, let that go and feel a deepness in the mind's eye. An overwhelming sense of Mother Goddess in the mind's eye. What is the brief this Mother Goddess brings into focus? Does it feel more controlling?*

*How does she teach man about man, then? Is she like a sheep dog harrying her sheep, nipping them at the ankles to keep them in line? And if they get away, how does she make them balanced again? Does all hell break loose? Do the heavens open? Is the Earth rent asunder; and man crushed into Order? Man trembles?*

*Now, God the Father, the Gods and Goddesses, God the Mother, each balanced man's ego in different ways, didn't they? But in the original Garden of Eden, God was what?*

*Feel a Garden of Contentment suddenly in the mind's eye. An idyllic garden of dreams, and countryside that ripples and flows and creates a sense of contentment that man was able to achieve before the Fall; a flourish of trumpets announces that this is God's Dream of Mankind unfolding.*

*In the Garden He is unseen, unheard, and unashamedly un-macho about His Dream of Mankind. He allows man to become man in his own way, in his own time and in the sense that man would be his own Master eventually, without the interference of God.*

*He was not in the business of balancing man, but of allowing man to develop, unfold in the glory of Godliness; in other words to become man in the changing image of God.*

*Sense the idea of the blossoming of man, making creative choices in that unfolding, like the branches of a flower, an organic and vigorous process. And alongside that, begin to sense the intervention of Eve who began to be aware of God's dream and was absolutely determined to eat of the Tree of Knowledge.*

*She made Adam eat the apple to satisfy her own need to acknowledge knowledge about the life of man, unable simply to accept the simple unfolding of man's creativity. So man was manifestly driven to knowledge about human creativity, as opposed to just letting it be held in the innocence of God's dreaming state.*

*Now feel the Garden of Eden in the Earth now. What does God feel like in the Garden of Eden? Where is God? Can you sense that God on Earth is part of all the growing, all the plant life; the flora and fauna is God-like? Man can be part of a state of union with the Earth, too.*

*So how must man balance himself to become part of that union with God in Earth? Not through God's intervention, because God is already in the Earth. The intervention of Eve brought knowledge of God and man, but it is time now to cast aside knowledge as an irrelevance, and to seek God within the garden. The God Within IS. He doesn't need to be understood, but experienced as the Divine in the Earth. He is in a new place now, isn't he?*

*So what is the thing most necessary to change the face of God now? To let go everything you know, old structures, old perceptions of God; all the cobwebs of a fading knowledge base, to let go old leadership and hierarchies.*

*And then what happens to God? God is released from that earlier judgmental stage and all other phases and faces of God, to allow a fuller investment in this new manifestation of God on Earth and within us all.*

We suggest the most valuable means of letting go the past is to really unleash the rage in which the mother has encapsulated us since time immemorial. We feel the most valuable thing to let go is the rage in each of us that is the rage of the Mother Earth, that her children were 'infected' by another source other than her own kind, as it were.

We feel the rage of the Earth is the most significant thing to understand now in terms of releasing all that is not of value to our well being. May we suggest the way to get to the rage of Mother Earth is to understand the level of rage inside our own feminine being (in man or woman) and to really accept the rage as part of a primal need in the first instance and then to release it as a totally incompatible part of us in the future.

May we feel into the most incredible rage for you, in that womankind holds the most dreadful rage that denounces life on Earth as an aberration? There is a primal rage inside all mankind. It is the rage of the ages that made us able to take care of ourselves physically at the dawn of time, but is now totally incompatible with our Divine inspirational nature.

The Earth was infused with primal rage that man should deign to enter her atmosphere. Her rage was instilled into man at the instinctive level for survival of the fittest levels of natural selection and to keep the male in touch with the child, who at that time he did not realise came from his own loins. By creating the rage of the mother in the man, Mother Earth kept the woman subservient to the man and therefore able to keep looking after the child of the union.

May we suggest something apocryphal now, in that we feel in each mother is the rage of the mother who did not want her child on Earth. Inside each mother is a love for the child and also a hatred of that child because the primal rage of the mother is in all of us, men and women.

In the past this rage was projected on to the male being, and in his turn he has adopted that level of primal rage which is a rage against the mother for hating him, as well as loving him. All very complex!

However in the coming times it is vital for the man to release his raging, in order for the raging mother to be released and allow the child to be born into a feeling of peace, security and love. Most children are born to mothers who wish their child to be their mirror.

All children then have their own rage to deal with at the primal level. Most children have a karmic history to complete in this life, so that all children in future may be born free of that complex mixture of love and hatred for the mother, by the mother and of the mother.

In the coming times the task is to let go that level of primal rage in order for the child to be free to become a being of pure divine Light on Earth. If the male disconnects from that primal level of rage on Earth, he will free the feminine to become a repository for any children born, without the need to hold it to a level of rage and hatred that is in every human being at the Earth level of experience.

*     *     *

*May we suggest you take an apple now and eat the outside, but leave the core to the birds. Eating the apple of knowledge but leaving the core to the birds is the way the woman of knowledge made herself the most incredible rod for her back.*

*May we suggest you take the apple again and eat it right down to the core and then eat the core. What is the difference between eating the full apple of knowledge rather than just eating it to the core? We feel the answer to that is the most amazing conundrum in human history. May we show you?*

*We feel the meditation needs to be done in the garden, if possible. Make a space on the grass, or the patio, to be the place you wish to make the garden of Eden. Don't worry about noise or aeroplanes going overhead, because the garden of Eden didn't have such difficulties. If you cannot be in the garden imagine yourself in some such Eden in your room.*

*Now feel yourself becoming immersed in the garden place by closing your eyes and imagining yourself in a dreamy state in the Garden of Eden, making yourself busy in the way the dream state busies itself, by feeling yourself innocently creating life in the way the dream state creates life.*

*Become aware of the tempting by Eve of Adam to eat the apple right now. She puts the apple in Adam's hand. Will he be able to make her happy by eating the apple? Does he sense trouble in making her happy? Feel how happy he's been with Eve and if the apple of knowledge is eaten, what will happen to their relationship?*

*Prior to the apple, life is a sensuous experience, you feel everything. You are innocent, but conscious of everything in a sensory way throughout your being, not in a mind way. You don't <u>know</u> about trees for example, but you <u>feel</u> them.*

*Eating the apple is a sell-out. Knowledge and mind means univer-*

*sities and hierarchies and cleverness. A loss of 'knowing it all'
inside the being.*

*But now, sense that Adam ate the apple, but not quite all of it. And
so he couldn't please Eve totally could he? Why is that relevant?
The male couldn't quite swallow it, could he? So in eating the tree
of knowledge Adam kept some information back so to speak, in his
cells.*

*What did he keep back in his cells? Mankind didn't give everything
up, did he? Man held on to his longing for the dream. To make it
real in Earth. Man's longing for a return to innocence was
incarnated on Earth, we suggest.*

And now that longing <u>not</u> to know anything is in the ascendant
again, isn't it? A longing to <u>feel</u> life again, not emotionally, but
sensuously. Feeling with the eyes open. A conscious feeling of life,
which is different from the original Garden of Eden because <u>that</u>
was an unconscious dream.

The journey away and the journey back is about coming back and
looking at what has always been there with a completely new
vision; a completely different understanding. To see in each living
thing the love that creation has given and receives with newness.
And yet the original dream seems very different because the illusion
will be broken.

# Chapter Four

# *PUTTING A PARTNER INTO THE EQUATION*

Do you have a partner? This chapter will help you make the right choice in partner if not. Mostly it is for those who have a partner in life right now, and is meant to help such a partnership survive the rigours and strains of being human. We feel a partnership is indeed the greatest place to learn what it is to be a human being on the planet at this particular time.

May we ask whether or not you love your partner? Naturally you think you do and we are not going to disagree with you on that score. What we want to delve into perhaps more fully, is what kind of love are you offering to this human being in your life.

Is it emotional love which tells you more about your needs in life than in love per se, or can you feel a deep deep commitment to allowing the partner to live his own life to the absolute fullness of his being? Think about it and raise a hand if you can honestly say that this is what your love is about; allowing that partner to become fully, truly who they are meant to be in this lifetime. May we show you the difference?

*Make a little boat out of a piece of paper. It doesn't need to be a brilliant piece of artwork, just something resembling a boat that will float on a dish of water. Make sure the boat is seaworthy so you can build into your sailboat a little self confidence that it won't sink to the bottom of the sea.*

*The boat is representing you on the sea of life right now. Make the boat as big or as small as you like, that's immaterial, but what is important is that you feel confident in its ability to float.*

*Take your boat to the bathroom and fill either the bath, or basin, with as much water as you feel you need to allow your boat a good amount to sail on. Take your boat into your right hand and push it off from the side now.*

*Feel the boat leave your hands and take a note of what that feels like right now; to feel your boat leaving the side, out of your control and into the depths of the 'sea'. Let the boat sail away out of the harbour and into the middle of the ocean.*

*Make sure the boat is looking safe now but don't touch it any more because this is you on the sea of life, bobbing and ducking on the sea of life, like human beings do in life. Make sure the boat feels okay, however, and if not, do replace it with something more stable. We don't want any shipwrecks at this stage.*

*Return to the other room you were in and take another piece of paper now and make it into another boat that feels just as strong in texture, just as remarkable in its ingenuity as you work at it, and then feel its quality of being 'not you' but the partner you want in life.*

*The partner you want to come across on the great sea of life. Is this possible? To feel in that other boat a sense of 'other' in your life? Feel its 'otherness' very strongly because it will need to feel like 'not you' when you enter it into your space on that sea of life in the bathroom.*

*Now, let's take the new boat into the bathroom and feel what it's like to place it in the water with the 'you' boat already there. Make a haphazard guess where to place the boat in relation to yours and accept that this is the partner in your life floating towards or around or beside you, right now.*

*What does that make you feel suddenly? Make an effort to get a real 'belly' reaction to how it feels as your own boat begins to make a connection in some way to that other boat. Any ideas? Make a real effort to sense the reaction you have to that other boat now. Really feel it deep down. What is going on in your body to tell you what you feel about that other boat?*

*Maybe the feeling is one of isolation because the boat doesn't appear to want to become involved with your boat after all. Maybe it's a feeling of elation because the boat is making you feel very very safe suddenly. Maybe the boat is taking itself off to the other side of the basin because you feel the whole idea of partnership with another boat is most undignified.*

*<u>Whatever</u> you feel when you watch the two boats together is what you feel about relationship. Trust that.*

Making the effort to establish your feelings about relationship <u>right now</u> is the place to start your exploration about partnerships in general, and yours in particular, isn't it?

It's a starting point for you to look at what relationship is truly about for you and begin to look at what it might be for you when all sorts of other considerations are taken into account and dismissed from the relationship arena.

So the way we see partnership is the way we begin to allow ourselves the luxury of making changes to our lives in regard to the most fundamental principles of cause and effect. What we reap from life depends on how we sow into life; it's as simple as that. Moment by moment we are making decisions about what we wish to get out of life, without making the direct acknowledgement that there will always be a repercussion if we only <u>need</u> in relation to someone else rather than be prepared to <u>give</u> in return. May we show you what we mean?

*Make a fist now. Take the fist in your other hand and check what that fist feels like to the hand it is now in. Make a fist with the other hand and take this in the first hand. What does that feel like? Any different? We're sure it does feel different one to the other. How?*

*Make a judgement about one fist by the other, in some way. What is one fist 'saying' to the other? May we suggest there is a 'needy' hand and a 'taking' hand, while the other is a 'giving' hand and a 'loving' hand. Is this possible?*

*Right and left hands are indicators of the two sides of ourselves; the masculine side on the right and the feminine side on the left. Make a note which side is needy, masculine or feminine, which side is giving. It isn't necessarily the masculine who gives or receives, or the feminine who gives and receives. It can be either.*

Now let's look at giving and receiving in detail. May we ask our readers to really listen to this aspect of partnership because giving and receiving are the fundamental cornerstones of 'cause and effect' lifetimes.

Make a decision now to really understand why giving and receiving are such powerful tools to a happy and healthy lifestyle with or without a partner, but particularly with of course.

Giving sounds as if it's the real clue to a happy lifetime. That's what most religious organisations would tell you. To give and not to count the cost is a well known adage indeed. But believe it or not, it is far harder to receive for most people than to give; and by receiving we mean that, at the most fundamental level, human beings feel guilty about being given things 'free'.

Maybe the journalists among you are always being given things 'buckshee' and you feel no remorse in accepting things, but in fact at a much deeper level, particularly in terms of relationships, most people do not receive gracefully.

Even if it looks as though a partnership is going all one way, with one partner giving endlessly to the other who seems to take it all as if by right, at a fundamental level a human being will feel guilty about such behaviour and pile on agonising amounts of unexpressed rage at feeling so guilty.

This will set up a huge level of resentment in both parties and the partnership will never be able to function in an amicable fashion, not because the one giving feels resentful, although they might, but because the one receiving is riddled with anxiety and guilt.

Receiving then, is the hardest thing in the world to achieve. It is feminine to receive and it is the feminine in both men and women that does the receiving. And it is this that makes it so difficult. The underlying nature of women is to receive yet because the imprint of mother, being the one who wounds us, is so strong, the 'mother' in all of us finds it absolutely impossible to feel in touch with her need to receive; rather than feel guilty about all the pain she has caused to her offspring over millennia.

Of course in some ways it is far more important that the woman herself learns to understand the mechanism of receiving because sexually she needs to be the partner who 'submits' to the thrust, the giving of the man who in turn needs to really feel that level of 'submission' in order to take great care over his modus operandi sexually. In other words there is a lot to learn about sexuality which begins with an understanding of how to receive in life.

Receiving comes from a new relationship to love which in our view is hardly understood at all in the modern world of today. Love is a dirty word in many households because it has been accompanied by the most unholy abuse seen for decades and decades in recent years. Love, in the conventional sense, often meaning a licence consciously or unconsciously to abuse the person who is the most precious object of love in your life.

This is because the real hatred of receiving reaches such horrendous proportions we can hardly begin to tell you how damaging it is to most couples on the planet. The minute someone is incapable of receiving from someone else a barrier is set up between them and abuse at one level or another is set in train. May we show you what we mean?

*Take a seat in the sitting room and find a place that feels really appropriate to do so. Let yourself feel around the room first in order to 'feng shui' the situation. In other words do make an effort to find the place that is absolutely 'right' to sit in right now. Don't worry if it feels as though someone else has more of a right to sit there, a mother or child or whoever, just take that seat anyway.*

*Listen to yourself as you make the decision where to sit. Is it okay, must I really choose now? How come this is so difficult to decide where to sit? Decisions, decisions. Whatever you find yourself thinking, in this effort to really find the right seat, note down before you actually sit in the seat.*

*Now tell someone else in your house that you are wanting to sit in this seat and ask them what they feel about it. For the sake of the exercise tell the person that in some ways they are perfectly at liberty to want to sit in that particular seat themselves, but to really really decide where they would 'most' want to sit because this is really and truly the place you have chosen to sit out of all other places in the room. Watch them looking around and feel the most incredible tension inside the solar plexus as you feel what would happen if they did decide to choose the place you are sitting in now.*

*Can you feel the incredible unease because someone might want your seat in the room at this moment? Can you feel the panic almost in some way? Wait a moment while the person is looking round carefully to choose their place in the room and ask them to make a concerted effort not to choose your place if they can. But to choose whichever one they want most of all now you've asked them to do so.*

*What do they do? One thing's for certain. Unless we're very much mistaken most people will never ever take the seat you have chosen. Why? Because the necessity not to receive, or rather only to give, is so deeply ingrained that the person would rather die than take your seat away.*

*However, what does that do to the person who has chosen not to take your seat. In our view the guilt begins to rise up and choke him in some way. A barrier is set up between the most willing giver, the other person and the lesser willing but nonetheless determined giver, you, because that other person feels guilty about not having taken the generous gift you have offered, the seat that means most to you in the room.*

*May we suggest the barrier is in some ways like a knock on the head, it sends a shock wave around the body and makes both parties feel discomforted in the room. Neither place seems right after all, does it?*

May we suggest the way forward now will be to accept that no one finds receiving easy. And yet, as we say, it is the single most important aspect of human life that we need to accomplish if the next stage of humanity is to arise naturally without more bloodshed and abuse, which is steadily increasing as more and more 'doing unto' is manifest into bloody and systematic abuse of the Earth herself.

What people do not understand is that the Earth herself has been unable to receive the incoming spiritual aspect of the universe and it is her guilt that allows such enduring pain to be inflicted on her. This may sound unbelievable in the extreme but Nature is by no means the only one to be hurt in this equation.

Man is feeling extremely agitated because the Earth cannot yet accept the spirituality that will enable her to speak her truth to those who are willing to hear.

Now, let us feel into how to receive in a very new way that has never been recognised on the planet before. In other words to achieve a level of feminine intuition that no one would understand to be the way the world needs to respond to life now, rather than understanding the world with the mind.

Life needs to be received in the most incredible way possible now, not acted upon by people who use their masculine arm, so to speak, by making gifts to the universe. Instead by receiving the universe man can begin to understand all there is to know about how he and Mother Earth and all that is, IS.

Receiving is a sexual response to the incoming energetic framework that will inform the planet in the coming years. A feminine sexuality is required that will show the way of the incoming energetic influences. To receive in the ethers is mirrored by an ability to receive sexually by the woman in the partnership; even if it is a homosexual one.

The woman who receives is enhancing the ability of the universe to penetrate into our world, so she can understand the mechanism of how to receive such influences and turn them into information at the deepest level of understanding.

May we show a womanly response to the incoming energies in some way?

*Exercise 3 on tape* (*You will need a piece of material for this exercise*)

*Make a small hole in a spare piece of material if you can. Take the hole to be the vagina of the average woman in Britain but don't take too much notice of size, just the sense that the hole represents the mechanism by which all women can receive in a marvellously new way.*

*All men should take notice of the fact that size is immaterial to the way women can receive and if the penis is too small or too big then life itself is too small or too big. An average woman can accept the penis of almost any man, one way or another, and her ability to receive from him is not dependent on the size of the man's penis.*

*Now take two fingers into the mouth and moisten the fingers as if this penis is ready to be inserted into the vagina. Ask yourself am I ready to receive now? Feel the feelings of really asking if you are ready to receive the universe through the vagina, and listen to the response.*

*If the response is negative don't worry. Wait a moment and become aware that more and more and more, you are becoming ready to receive 'all that is' through the vagina now.*

*'All that is' is worth waiting for, isn't it? So let the vagina, the hole, represent the way in to receiving 'all that is' through that vagina. Make a magnificent gesture of surrender now inside yourself.*

*Perhaps a beautiful ring appears in your mind's eye, perhaps a feeling of love surrounds you. Perhaps you are feeling the extent you wish to surrender and pick a symbol in your mind's eye to represent the quality of your surrender to 'all that is'.*

*Now make the decision that in some way your partner is about to offer you the universe through love making. It means he is absolutely giving you everything he has to give right now and YOU ARE AGREEING TO RECEIVE IT, NO HESITATION, JUST TO RECEIVE FROM HIM once in your life, totally and fully wishing to receive.*

*Make a decision that in the coming minutes your wish to receive overpowers all other decisions not to receive. Make the decision to do so now. To receive now and be done with it. Make the decision to make yourself look and feel as silly as it takes to receive fully for the first time in your life. Okay?*

*Now take the two fingers you have licked to represent the penis and closing your eyes, put the two fingers through the hole you have made in the cloth. Imagine whatever you like in this regard but remember this is a loving, loving, giving, penis that wants only that you should receive all that there is to receive.*

*Make yourself feel that amount of giving in some way and at the same time really lay back and instead of thinking of England, for a change let yourself really really RECEIVE in some way that cannot be mistaken for anything else.*

*Lay back and really receive that penis in the most joyous, receiving way possible to you. Let the penis feel like the most giving loving accommodating penis you ever felt in your life, making sure the penis is really in the opening that is your vagina, however big or small it is, because that penis only wants for you to receive now; nothing else in the world is more important than that you should receive him, and by definition, all there is to give. How else can man receive 'all that is' without feeling he is <u>receiving</u> 'all that is'?*

*Now become the penis suddenly. Become the penis that is pushing its way into the vagina now in such an incredibly loving, giving, massaging manner and feel what it's like to be giving everything there is to give to the woman you are part of, in this mode of giving.*

*What is the most overwhelming feeling you have in this incredible moment of giving? Is it just possible that the feeling is of receiving? Unashamed and unabashed receiving, in some way?*

*A different way than you have ever experienced before in love making, a less thrusting receiving, a more receptive receiving than you imagined might be possible in the love making you know and love? Can it be that in giving all there is to give, there is a reciprocal and beautiful ability to receive? Is there?*

*And in that level of receiving through giving, how does that make you feel about the woman in front of you now? The woman you thought you loved so deeply, but in fact, judging from the boat exercise, you actually have an enormous sense of misgiving over.*

*What can you say about this woman who has been receiving to the extent that she surrendered totally to that receiving and therefore surrendered totally, for once in a lifetime to you; without guilt, without barriers, without wanting to dive for cover into the bushes of embarrassment, without resentment at such surrender?*

May we suggest most sincerely that a real relationship is one of being able to receive at the highest level of input from the Divine. God has made man in His own image but on Earth that image is divided into masculine and feminine essences. In the male there is a divine spark of feminine; in the female there is a divine spark of masculine.

In love-making those divine sparks are able to meet in the sacral region and rise upwards towards the spiritual source, then downwards into the ground of Divine integration at the deepest sacred level that human beings can reach.

A fountain of energetic resonance between Heaven and Earth can be released so that the act of love-making itself is representative of that Divine relationship between matter and spirit on Earth.

May we suggest that indeed this is the purpose of love making in the New Age where procreation is no longer the only purpose for making love between two distinct, separate and integrated human beings.

Love making can become the very symbol of Divine Union of Heaven and Earth. God incarnate within each symbiotic and separate couple who choose to undertake the sacred task of Dyadic relationship.

Dyadic relationship is unusual in that it does not need to be based on emotional need between two people, but the most exquisite freedom to choose to conduct a relationship within the confines of 'one to one' expression; yet conducted primarily for the collective to understand and appreciate the Divine Gift, Heaven on Earth.

As more and more couples become clearer and clearer in their own relationship to themselves, and to the Divine Spark within, so will relationship become a clearer and clearer expression of God on Earth. Two people who have chosen to become who they are within a relationship that ultimately will express who God is to the world. No mean feat, huh?

So, how does the relationship become one of such beauty and contribution? For the most part it is about receiving and allowing. Allowing that other person to become who they are in whatever way they are able to become that being of Light that expresses a part of the Divine principle on Earth. Receiving that person as they are, in the way they choose to be, is ultimately the goal of each partner in a relationship.

However that does not mean receiving all the incoming emotional clutter that each of us comes into existence carrying like a burden on our shoulders. No indeed!

That is the responsibility of each individual to clear and clarify before there is any possibility of making the grade as a carrier of God's divine spark. No mean feat again, is it? To take responsibility for that level of clarity that enables a relationship to function at the highest level of God's will to be incarnated on Earth.

Mother and father, daughter and son. All the information is carried within our relationships in this life. Although past life recall can aid and abet the unleashing of the patterns in which we bury our true selves, all that is required to let go such blockages and miseries is held in the relationships we undergo in this particular life, come what may. All the intricacies of that unblocking can be perceived within our own lifetime's intimacies; whether with friends, mother, lover.

All we need to know about our dysfunctional selves can be read like a book in the way our lives play out before us. No one need go further than the last conversation with someone they love to read the mask that is covering the clarity of Divine wisdom. Try it and see.

Any conversation with your lover that leaves you unhappy tells you something about the blocks that are waiting to be released. For example, your partner decides to go ahead and dig up part of your precious garden in order to grow more vegetables. He hasn't asked your opinion although in some ways you don't really care that much; it's more that he hasn't respected your need to take control over your environment in order to become the one who makes the decisions. Apart from that he has taken more ground than he said he would. What is your problem?

May we suggest the way forward is to decide whether or not it is really a problem, or whether it is just futile nit-picking because he hasn't paid respect to your needs and feelings? Respect for your needs and feelings. Respect. That's the point, not the garden at all. The garden is simply allowing the issue of respect to be highlighted in the most immediate sense of arguing round and round the garden issue.

*What can you do to release the hurt that the partner is unable to show you a level of respect that you feel is due to you, even though you didn't know that this was such a burning problem for you?*

*Make a decision not to argue about the garden but to draw a picture of non-respect in some way. Maybe a donkey who is being sidelined because a horse has come into the field to be petted. Or a piece of paper being turned into a boat that ultimately is ignored by that other piece of paper turned into a boat. Whatever comes to the mind's eye when you feel the feeling about the digging up of the garden.*

*Feel the disrespect deeply and find a way of making that disrespect a more manageable size. Then take the drawing to the partner and say, 'This is how I feel over the garden'. Discuss the feelings about the drawing and then ask the partner to draw a picture of his feelings about that plot of land.*

*Is the feeling anything at all to do with disrespect, or is it merely a feeling of becoming more who he is in this life, more of who he wants to be, to become a meaningful human being on the Earth?*

*May we suggest that all relationships are built on a need to be seen in some way and the most obvious way to do that is impose some level of power structure over the relationship. May we suggest that once the issue of respect has been dealt with a new meaning can become evident in the issue of the garden.*

*Once the gardener sees his own relationship to the issue, that of needing to express himself creatively, the non-gardener has to respect that, however much it hurts to allow the gardener to do unattractive things, as they see it.*

*Now, what about you? Why can't you find something else to seize on in terms of what is the matter at this moment? A sense of needing to be seen, to express yourself too in a manner that suits you more than gardening does, but equally to the way in which gardening does to your partner. Find out what is the problem deep down now, over and beyond respect and beyond the garden. What is the issue most concerning you right now?*

*May we suggest you now draw a picture that represents how you are feeling at this moment about the garden as a whole. Let it really express your innermost feeling right now. Find an expression to sum up your feeling and make that the centre of your focus.*

*Change the image from garden to workplace and see how that makes you feel now. What is it that would make your heart sing now? Recognise the situation that you find most creative now and allow the gardener to become what he needs to be in the garden, while you find the way to what makes your heart sing.*

All you need do to find your most intimate relationship to the Self is find out what makes the heart sing; and everything that happens to block it is meant to be seen and released. May we suggest the relationship brings up all you need to know about those blockages and in many ways it can be resolved within the relationship if the two people concerned will take time to talk in pictures in this way.

Most people understand the psychology of inner development in this way, but in our view there is far more self help available if both partners will take time out to work on their material together like this.

Drawing pictures of situations from the feeling level, not just the head level, is one way of avoiding psychiatrists and reaching an understanding about the Self and Other in the most rewarding manner, without resorting to shouting and raging over every little thing that offends and upsets you about the other person.

May we suggest the next time you have an upset you sit down with your pencil and paper and sketch out the consequences of that upset – whatever it may be – and allow yourself to discover far more about yourself than you might imagine.

Allow your imagination to run away with you and you will discover the richness of your current psychological patterns in order to release the burden you carry from birth.

In partnership all the issues are possible and all the issues are solvable, provided you understand that the point of it all is to wish for the highest in yourself and the best in your partner.

## Chapter Five

# REMEMBERING HOW TO BECOME A TREE OR PLANT

In days of old, men and women were able to commune with Nature in such a way that Nature told them what their lives were about from day to day to day. Man and Nature were in league with each other and the Gods came and went, in time to the rhythms and cycles of Nature.

Mars was the God of War, but in natural terms Mars was the bringer of fire. Venus was the Goddess of Love, but in natural terms she brought the ability to appreciate beauty in Nature.

Mercury was the God of lightning communication, but in the nature of things he was the bringer of light to the minds of men in order to do things in the most natural way possible, in touch with the rhythms and nature of man and his environment.

So where did it all go, do you suppose? May we suggest the natural rhythm of Nature was disturbed by man, in order to become a reflective being of his own nature.

When man was in touch with Nature in an instinctive fashion he was able to respond at a cellular level to the nature of time and cycles of Nature. Now, though, in his ability to reflect, he is given a level of responsibility for his actions that he has never had before.

The introduction of psychology in the earlier part of the century was a symbol of the way man and his natural rhythms, were becoming vassal to the way man thought about himself.

In the beginning when man's thoughts were only for himself in relation to Nature, the world was evolving slowly but surely towards the time when man would become aware of himself in the act of becoming.

Now that man is able to self-reflect, he is more and more able to take responsibility for his own becoming, and in that becoming man has become almost totally oblivious to his true relationship to Nature.

However, the pendulum must swing and in our view the most important message we wish to convey in this book is that 'in time is Nature' and 'in Nature there is time'.

May we explain what we mean? We feel the most significant change over the last few decades is the sense that man is not here merely to reproduce his own nature but also to take care of the other aspects of Nature of which his environment consists.

Man is not alone any more in the way he became convinced he was. Through the Industrial Revolution, particularly, he was made invincible by the sense that man could create all he required in the world through the manipulation of the resources provided by God.

Now, however, man is becoming aware that what God gave for man's pleasure no longer exists in the enormous quantities required, if man is to consume at the rate he has been consuming over the last two hundred years.

What we want to convey in this book is that to be happy, man has only to reflect on the life he has right now and to stop wishing for a life he cannot possibly sustain at the rate resources are dwindling.

Who can help him see the folly of these ways, and how to take the consumption out of the way he views his place in the world now? Why, Nature herself. Or himself. Or itself.

All three views of Nature are viable and indeed valuable as a means of relinquishing the misnomer that Earth is only feminine; to be ravaged and pillaged in the fashion she has been over the last centuries.

Man is man in Earth as well as in mind and spirit. Man is now able to understand Earth in terms that the ancients could only aspire to in their instinctive understanding of Nature and her wiles.

Man can now reflect on his own situation in regard to Nature and can indeed reflect on himself in his own environment to <u>understand</u> the whole of Nature within himself. He can be the instrument of Nature's understanding her own need to become a conscious being with needs and metaphors of behaviour of her own.

May we suggest that in due time man – and we mean the male within all of us – will be able to relate to Earth as a conscious, sensate being who can speak its woes and troubles and who, we hope, will be heard in a manner unthinkable since those ancient days.

Man will no longer be directed from 'on high' by a male God whose wishes are turned into judgements by the male mindedness of power and position, but from below by a male Earth awareness that man is but a pawn in the game of Heaven and Earth and has been a co-respondent in the divorce proceedings between spirit and matter.

Now however, the way forward is to understand the meaning of the pawn in terms of the groundsman who is in the game in order to stay the execution of the King for as long as possible.

In our view man is here now to understand the relationship between Heaven and Earth on the planet and to carry out to the best of his ability his task of mediating so that ultimately the God of Heaven can respond in space-time to the rhythms and cycles of Earth time.

Now that man is self-reflective he can mediate between Heaven and

Earth by understanding his own relationship to the spirit and matter of Godliness in his own being.

Many people have been driven into the spotlight by making a huge song and dance of relating to the spiritual aspects in life; cult figures who often cause enormous disruption to the lives and families of those they attract.

What they have missed is the enormous potential of simply being human on this planet at this time, in this way. No need to take a space ship to comet Hale Bop at all. All that needs to be done is to take a moment to contemplate a tree nearby and ask the tree its meaning in the scheme of things and then build up a picture of your relationship to that meaningful exchange you have had with the tree.

Take a willow tree for example. A willow tree will tell you of the value of the unconscious within you, to bring out the whole truth and nothing but the truth of your historical relationship to the darkness within you. Darkness which is, in fact, the blessing you have arrived with, in order to push your way to the light of God on Earth.

The marigold is a flower of exquisite beauty indeed, because it allows you to feel inside a very deep connection to the heart of a matter you are contemplating. Allow the marigold to enter your heart and place a problem you are facing into that marigold in your heart. Hear what marigold has to say about the situation; heart-felt, and deal with the matter accordingly.

\*     \*     \*

In our view the most spectacular changes are about to manifest themselves in the way we look at Nature. Nature will become the most meticulous teacher on Earth. The Earth has suffered enormously through the thoughtlessness of man, but in our view this is only half the story. May we tell you a tale of Earth now?

Once upon a time the Earth was full of hatred for mankind. Why? Because she felt the most inordinate pressure to become the mother of man rather than to continue the journey to the magnificence of matter. Matter, you will recall, is only half the story of man's sojourn on Earth.

Man is made in God's image and it is for this purpose he is incarnated on the planet where all manifesting beings learn to become a human after many many lives in the etheric realms of other dimensional realities. Earth is the final step, if you like, in the evolutionary cycle of entities that descend from God's worlds.

It is on Earth that all the information is stored about the universes that comprise God's incarnational dream, as it were. Earth is the place where all beings are capable of knowing the entire history of the universe simply by existing in the humanity they were born with.

In other words, man is the repository of everything that ever was and ever shall be, did he but know it and there is no need for the fraternity of men you call scientists to seek endlessly beyond the material world to discover 'all that is'. It is here, right here in every human being who uncovers the lock and finds the key to infinity.

So, in sum, man is a very very particular being isn't he? He can unlock the key to matter as well as to the universal realms of the spiritual ethic in the universe. May we add that man can also destroy everything that ever was and ever will be in the universe, so it is no wonder that when the lock was hidden the key was put miles away from it......just in case.

Many have found the lock, but very few find the key. But it is in the evolutionary scheme of things that man has come of age now and in the very near future the lock and key will become available to many more people on the planet; people who have struggled with their journey to Divine Meaning, who have so to speak, earned their laurels to become the first human beings on Earth plane to experience the full Divinity of mankind on Earth – and to understand the most incredible secrets of Divine Law as God descended is able to do.

May we therefore, suggest that Earth herself was very reluctant to accept man into her realms of experience. She felt the disruption of man would be far too great and in her wisdom rejected the idea of man in principle.

In other words 'ideas', in the Platonic sense, begin in the etheric realms of reality and are transposed into matter through the workings of the devic kingdoms on Earth. Devas are the makers, the weavers of form into earthly reality.

May we suggest that when the Moon beings, a diffuse reflection of the original Sun beings, returned to the Earth in the first universe, as it will be called, the 'sons of God mated with the daughters of men', so that the combined forces of spirit and matter were instigated in the new Earth man. Sexual reproduction was the means by which this cross-bred mutation would be manifest in the future universe.

In the second universe, the big bang, as scientists describe it, out of a dense black hole into which the first universe had imploded, man was becoming more established in the Earth plane, although in some ways he was further behind than he was in Universe One.

May we suggest that in the second universe the natural evolution of man was from the sea to the land in one great jump of evolutionary by-passing. We mean by this that man became the humanoid we know today only through the evolutionary endeavours of the fish community which knew inside its pattern of destiny that it would evolve into man, in order for man to understand its position in Earth as well as in the order of the universal scheme of things. It was then that Earth rebelled.

Earth was not ready for man in some ways. She felt the imprint of man very heavily on her etheric make-up. Man would be the dominant factor on Earth because he alone was capable of manifesting spirit into matter and she was incapable of allowing man's free will to become the arbiter of her destiny.

It was she, and then every mother, who rejected her child, in terms of making each man, woman and child on Earth feel betrayed, rejected, abandoned, abused or denied. Remember what we said in an earlier chapter; that mother is the scapegoat for our innate feelings of rejection.

Mother Earth rejected man-child on Earth. And man being man inherently felt he must conquer the conqueror inside and outside himself. Man was inherently able to feel himself the victim to Earth so he began systematically to destroy her. Mostly by war.

Man is programmed to go to war and always will be until he lets go the level of rage he carries against mother. Mother symbolises all that is powerful and vengeful, and unless this state of affairs changes man will always be in conflict with himself and others.

Many people only look at ecology in terms of man's rage against Nature, but it must become clear to all concerned that mother is the instigator of primal rage not man. All mothers, at the deepest deepest level of their primal being, do not want a child to be born to Earth. Man's rage against man is merely the outcome of man's rage against mother and mother's rage in rejecting him.

Paradoxically, of course, mothers love and adore their children; they are bound to them in the most intrinsic ways as animals are to their offspring. Mother Earth at her primal instinctual level cannot bear not to have a child because reproduction of Self is absolute within the primal Earth plane.

So, we are beginning in this stage of evolution to witness the incredible paradox between love and hate. Witness the amount of sexual, emotional and spiritual abuse of our children today. No one can believe how a mother or father can abuse a child to the degree that so many are being abused today. This is the outcome of a need to release the mother's rage at her Earth children and become aware of the enormous benefit her children can offer her, when they are in turn able to let go the rage inside themselves.

Rage is becoming paramount inside most men today. Maybe they are able to suppress it, but believe us, most men are becoming incapable of holding on to the sense of primal rage that is bellowing up from the ancient memory of Earth Mother rejection.

As man becomes more 'rarefied' energetically, as the atmosphere on the Earth plane becomes more conducive to the manifestly lighter energies invading the planet right now, all the ancient memories that have bogged man down into the Earth environment need to surface to be released.

Man is destined to become a repository of the most incredible methods of manifestation on the planet and the old forms need to let go their hold on man's imagination.

May we say here that energy and imagination are the building blocks of the universe and in the future man's imagination will know no bounds. In future man will imagine future without recourse to confines of the past, as he does now. In other words man's level of freedom to create his reality will leave 'virtual reality' standing.

Man's own ability to create life in his own image will become the most incredible route to life he has ever imagined. But God's plan is to allow man that level of freedom only when the old primal negative patterns of existence have been released and purified. Until then man will continue to labour under the illusion that he is the only manifest being in the universe who cannot feel free of life as he knows it now.

Our thesis for the book is that making the most of the life you've got is all you need do. It knows no bounds just as it is.

May we suggest a most valuable way of retreading our footsteps now is to really become acquainted with our Earth heritage in order to become aware that inside us is the whole universe.

May we offer an exercise in which you can really understand how man, in the sense of man who is woman and man, has denied himself the most wonderful experience of all time, that of making a connection to his root. And by root we mean that the root chakra of his being is mostly disconnected from the Earth plane. In fact, most human beings are not fully incarnated into their humanness at all, much less able to feel their Nature selves; the part of them that isn't Divine at all, but which now is becoming a server of Light nonetheless.

Man can mediate Light through to matter and allow a light to shine through the darkness of matter into the wonderful level of atomic structure where information is stored for anyone to see or feel or recognise with their being; not, we must emphasise, with their mind, in the way most people use mind.

'Light is the mind' is another way of describing matter. Mind is the light of matter. Not the intellectual mind that most scientists would have us believe is the route to knowledge, but the mind of Light mindedness. Light can penetrate the intensity of matter through mind. May we show you what we mean?

### *Exercise 4 on tape*

*Become aware that the wind is blowing through your hair now. Become aware that a light is shining on your face in some way unknown to you before. Take a moment to really understand the feeling of this light shining onto your face because this light is the light of the mind.*

*Mind that lights your face, not your brain cells, is really light of mindfulness. Mindfulness is the most beautiful mind in the universe. To be mindful of light is the task ahead of all humanity now.*

*Take the light of mind on your face and become aware that it begins to travel down your body, inside and outside the body now. It feels as though a beautiful sense of light, a shimmering sense of moonlight perhaps, is shimmering down through the body into the depth of your beingness.*

*Allow the light to settle deep down into the bowels of your being, the bowels of your body now, and feel the light making that part of your body feel free and warm right now.*

*Let the light of mind dwell in the base of your body now and feel its effect. Feel a warm glow radiating round the root of your body now and tell yourself how it feels now to feel the light of the mind radiating around the base of your being. Is it feeling light or manifesting discomfort?*

*Make the decision to allow it to become a beautiful sense of peace and comfort, not a nasty agitating feeling at all; a real sense of lightness in the base of the body because the light of the mind is now circulating freely through and down and round the body, isn't it?*

*Make the decision to really experience this feeling of light shimmering through and around and down the body now and don't question its effects at all, provided they are good, and easy on the being; not discomfort at all, just the sense of feeling bigger and more at ease and, well, lighted up in some gentle, fascinating manner that makes you want to become at one with the Earth plane now.*

*Make a decision to really understand the Earth as it wishes to express itself to you right now, within the framework of this lighted up sensation in the base of your body. Make a decision to really understand what Earth plane wishes to tell you in terms of a manner of behaviour that you might adopt for Earth plane's sake.*

*How is the Earth wishing you to behave in the future for her and your own sake? Ask the Earth to tell you what her meaning might be to you right now. Ask her. Tell her you wish to take a new view on how the Earth plane feels about you and herself.*

May we suggest the Earth is very eager to talk to you right now because she too is evolving into a sentient, conscious being; as James Lovelock of Gaia fame suggests.

May we really emphasise that in the future man – in terms of the male in men and women – will be able to listen to the Earth's sense of herself and what man might do in the future to support the increasing number of men and women alive on the planet.

Planet Earth is a truly creative creature in her own right and in the scheme of things it is most creative to support her and decongest her energy fields from the enormous amount of negativity that has built up over centuries of negative output, whether through man's inhumanity to man, or through the industrial wastes that pour into the environment.

No one knows better than Earth herself how to become a cleaner, more rarefied natural phenomenon that will carry the new consciousness into the next millennia. No one knows Earth like Earth knows Earth and she will make herself felt one way or another, come what may.

If we do not listen to her now she will throw off such negativity by rearranging large parts of her surface in order to do so. Let's begin to help her before she gets totally destroyed in the process.

May we suggest that in future man will be able to achieve the most incredible feats imaginable but to be able to tune into the Earth plane is by far the most significant part of the magnificent applications of his new skills and abilities in information gathering.

May we suggest that, in fact, the only way to make the real connections required of the new human being, can come from the Earth plane. Man is an Earth creature and although in future he will be able to manifest information from the whole universe, in fact his place is in the Earth plane, no more no less; and indeed it is with the Earth plane that he needs to become acquainted now.

Earth is, as we have said, the repository of 'all that is', and in Nature are the clues to many many of life's present difficulties.

May we remind the reader to read between the lines of what we say, rather than to distinguish letter by letter the content of the words. More important is to really understand the energy experience of these words, because man will only be able to sense his surroundings if he senses himself as a sensual creature not an intellectual one.

Man is becoming more and more sensitised to his surroundings, hence the enormous number of allergies that abound right now, but because he cannot manage to intellectualise about the solution he gives up on really taking the problem into his sensual mechanism and discovering how to make the situation better.

What we wish to explain to the reader is that mind is a fragile creature in terms of needing to accomplish a great many tasks now, not least to interpret all the signals coming into the planetary realm to be decoded into useful information.

May we suggest that sensitivity to these incoming signals is as much part of the dis-ease felt by so many people as the purely physical signs of dis-ease and it is now up to the sensual side of man to manifest more strongly in order to pick up the signals and interpret them within the framework of the human body.

One magnificent way of practising to use the sensory mechanism is to really tune into the plant and animal worlds in order to listen to their interpretation of the incoming signals. All plants and animals have the capacity to interpret their own vibrational messages, so to speak.

In other words, in our view what needs to be accomplished within the next few years is a strictly anthropomorphical relationship to the other kingdoms of Nature. They, too, understand that the nature of Earth's relationship to man is changing and they can be relied on to assist man to understand the changing nature of his world now.

Make a concerted effort to concentrate madly on the environment now in order to clear the airwaves between Nature and man, in order to understand how completely different man is becoming to himself.

Politicians would be well advised to remember the old adage 'a week is a long time in politics' because in the enormous shifts of this moment, a week is a long time in anyone's fixed understanding of life. If politics doesn't catch up with changing Nature, man will be denied his rights as a fully paid up member of the Universe Party.

Nature has an enormous amount to offer each and every one of us now in order to make the changes as comfortable as possible; otherwise as we say, the Earth will simply heave a sigh of resignation and tip off the world.

In our view a really valuable message to offer the people of the world is to make the effort now to complete the cycle of change in as elegant a way as possible. Elegance is something the natural world knows a lot about. Elegant living will allow man to understand the ways of Nature in the deepest sense of that word.

Make the most of your ability to be elegant in life; not in the material sense of buying more and more dresses, but in behaving elegantly to yourself and each other, in such a way that a sense of elegance can become the way of life in this world. Surely it isn't too much to ask to make the effort to maintain a level of elegance in the world?

May we suggest the way to feel elegant is to recognise the way Nature behaves? May we show you what we mean?

*Make the decision right now to understand the way Nature is an elegant matter. Make the decision to really feel the way Nature is able to reproduce itself over and over and over again, in such a way that life becomes an elegant series of monologues with God for each species on Earth.*

*The way to begin to understand the way Nature makes herself felt in the world is to feel a daisy in your hand now. Feel it very very carefully in your imagination. Take the daisy and carefully turn it over and over and over in your hand and feel the way the daisy enjoys your gentle caresses now.*

*Make the daisy feel welcome in your hand now and feel its nature begin to make itself felt in some way to your senses. Make the daisy feel really really welcome in some way by showing the daisy your warmest nature in whatever way you can. Feel a great love for this little daisy in your hand and feel its response to that level of love you are giving to it.*

*Now feel a response back from the daisy. Feel the way it can respond to your love in such a way that it begins to speak to you of its nature somehow. Allow the daisy to really open up to your heart in some way by listening to it through the heart.*

*Make the daisy very very welcome and feel its ability to choose to communicate with you in your heart now. Feel a lovely sense of the daisy's wish to tell you how it feels about you, first of all, and then begin to feel in your heart how the daisy feels about itself. Make sure the daisy feels welcome throughout, concentrate on the sense of caring for the daisy all the while so that you and it are in constant loving contact together.*

*Make it feel ready to begin to tell you how it feels about you, about itself and about...well the world in general. Get a sense of the daisy's conversation with you inside yourself and allow the sense of how the daisy feels to penetrate warmly inside you right now.*

*Tell the daisy it is appreciated very much for its contact with you. Now allow the feeling of that particular daisy to become a sense of something else. A sense of the daisy's manner of being in the world.*

*Make a decision to really feel that manner of being; a level of elegance in the world that will truly astonish you if you allow that daisy to penetrate your being with its beingness. Does that feel okay to allow the daisy to truly penetrate you with its elegance now?*

*Remember to become really aware of daisy's elegance now because in the fullness of time elegance can become the byword of a way of life that man has never known until now.*

Elegance is a very important word for the future of mankind as is the word integrity. Elegance and Integrity are the words of Nature that mankind needs to absorb into his own creative nature from now on.

Elegance and Integrity of form, of love of mankind itself in the new era of opulence that man can achieve for all of his kind in the nearest possible future, if only man would listen to what the world of matter has to tell us.

Make the decision today to really listen, to absorb and to love

Nature in its purest nature, not only by becoming the ardent ecologist – which of course we applaud – but more importantly to understand what Nature has to say on the subject of such ecological aspects of well-being on the planet. They may surprise you, but never disappoint.

Nature will thrive indeed if man can 'get off his perch' in the idea that humankind knows more than Nature does about the world it lives in, and make the commitment to listen for a change.

To listen and learn in a simple, mindful manner that will surprise you in its simplicity. Make the effort to hear what Nature says to you each day and act accordingly.

# Chapter Six

# *WHAT ABOUT THE WORKERS?*

Work is a serious issue in the world today. How many of you have decided either that the rat race is not worth the candle, or have been given no option but to find another route to the well-being you seek?

More and more people have been given little option but to withdraw from the money-making arena that has dominated the culture for so long now. It seems there was never any other method of measuring the quality of life than through money.

In fact there was. In the matriarchal era before the advent of the mind cultures of the patriarchal societies, little heed was paid of the amount people managed to accumulate in terms of wealth in the financial sense, or possessions in the cultural sense.

What we remember is the era of matriarchy in which family and friendship were what counted in terms of wealth of achievement. The matriarchal society allowed each individual to express his or her manifest creativity in such a way that the wealth was expressed in terms of friendship or family ties.

In other words, your wealth was your position in society in terms of what we described earlier as Elegance and Integrity. A state of being that allowed each person to become as creative and endearing as he could become in this one life.

May we suggest the life of the worker in this century has become intolerable in many ways that no one could have foreseen when the idea of full employment for each person in the country became fashionable.

In our view the most difficult thing to combat now is this sense that everyone should be guaranteed employment for the rest of their lives, and that if they don't keep working their quality of life will dramatically decline. This feeling is so set into the fabric of society now that anyone who does not fit into this constant working pattern, unless they are 'just a housewife', is considered sub-standard in some way. Aren't they? Aren't they? Think about it.

Doesn't it strike you as 'poor' if someone isn't committed to the work life of the times; and isn't it considered just a little 'low class' if a person isn't able to fulfil this norm that society has now instigated, to its cost, at all costs?

May we suggest that governments will be wrong to continue to pursue the dream of 'full employment for all', and pass on the idea to our readers that in fact full employment isn't 'the norm' anywhere else in the universe or even in the Nature kingdoms. What we are suggesting is that 'full play' is the norm and should be in all kingdoms of Nature, including man.

Full play. What do we mean by full play? How on Earth does full play get the bills paid and the mortgage sorted out? Well, it does. May we show you what we mean?

### Exercise 5 on tape

*Find a corner of your room that suggests itself to you as play school. Not a cluttered corner but the corner that in your mind's eye feels like a good place to play at playing. Now take a moment to feel into your corner to make sure it definitely is a place that you can play; not work at playing, but play itself, in some way as yet unfathomed.*

*Right, now take off your shoes and put them outside the play area if you can and feel the difference the play area makes you feel without your shoes on. Now take off your glasses if you have them; put them outside the play area and make a decision to really let go anything else in your mind but play.*

*It is important to really let go anything else from your mind, about this being silly or nonsense, or whatever your mind tells you to think about putting time aside to play.*

*Now make a circle in your imagination around yourself and take a sounding on how this makes you feel to have a circle around yourself in your play corner. Does it make you feel safer than if you didn't have a circle around you? Make sure the circle makes you feel safe.*

*Now, become aware of a small child in the circle with you who wants to play very much with you in your circle. Can you feel that child with you now? What is the child like who is now with you in your circle, who wants you to play with him or her? Speak to the child and find out what sort of play it wants to instigate with you now.*

*Is your child wanting to play hopscotch, or hide and seek or what? Can you feel into how your child likes to play in this circle of play right now? Is the child happy that you have decided to set this time aside to play, or is it scornful that you might not mean it? What does the child want you to do in order to start your game of play? To run and hide or make the first jump, or what?*

*Can you decide to do whatever your child says you should do if you are to play nicely with him or her? Can you? Can you hop? Or run and hide or skip? Play nicely with your child and see how that makes you feel suddenly, to hop or skip or hide or run away or....whatever. Can you feel what it's like to really play as a child?*

*Become aware of the way the child in you wants to play now. In what way does play become the modus operandi of your life now, in terms of how you play as the child at play right now? Is it by becoming a star in the play, or a person who simply gets on with the playing in a comfortable, easy manner in some way?*

*What is your need in the playing right now; to become the one who takes on all comers, or the one who settles down to become a player in the team, so to speak? How do you play in your life? What manner of play is the most significant to you in your life right now?*

*Now, make the decision to put yourself in the work corner of the room, right now. Put yourself in the corner of the room that represents most for you, in your mind's eye, the work corner of the room right now. Can you imagine yourself in that corner of the room feeling the way you do when you are at work, in whatever way that work is operating for you right now?*

*Go on then, find yourself in that corner of the room so that you can become aware of <u>how</u> you operate in the working environment. Place yourself, once more into a circle of safety in which to work out how you live in the work mode of your life.*

*Put yourself in the work circle right now, and become aware that you are now entering the way you work in the world. Don't feel yourself 'at work' so to speak, but in the world of work in general.*

*Allow yourself a few moments to centre down into yourself and become aware of a man in the corner of your circle. May we suggest this is a man, not a woman, in your circle. Feel his energy and make sure the energy is male, not female, because in our view it is the male in most human beings who 'goes to work', in the way most people choose to go to work today.*

*Now, feel the energy of this man and take a moment to describe it to yourself in terms of how it feels in quality of dynamism. Feel a sense of how this man works in the world of work. Feel his motivational drive, so to speak, and describe how he becomes aware of himself as a man of the world, to the world.*

*Make his sense of himself come into your own body and allow it to become you in some way that you realise you recognise as you right now. The you who goes to work to become something in the world of work.*

*Feel that man's manner of being in the world of work inside you now and allow it to permeate your beingness so that you really feel how you operate as the man in the world of work. How does it compare to the way of the child at play? Not half so refreshing or creative or passionate or..... meaningful, is it?*

*Why not? What in the child cries out to be acknowledged that the man has not fulfilled in you? What is it the child created that the man in you has not? Feel the yearning inside for what the child was able to provide that the adult you in the world of work did not provide. What is it, do you feel?*

*What can the child alone provide for the yearning in the adult world of work; a sense of fun, a sense of meaning that passes all understanding? A sense of living in the Now of life, unlike the man in the world of work who lives in the ever present future of his life, doesn't he?*

*Make the decision now to work in your corner as the child would choose to work now. Bring in the child into your work corner and make the decision to let him show you how to work now. Make the child the partner of the man in some way and watch them behave in a child and man sort of way in your work corner.*

*How does the child approach the man in your work corner right now? What is his manner of greeting the man in your work corner? What is his form of address, do you imagine? How is the man responding to the child's form of address?*

*Does he delight in it, in some way? Is he pleased to hear this form of address that the child is addressing him by? What is that form of address? Does it suit you more than the one you normally feel addressed by in the world of work? A 'self description' you have taken on in work terms?*

*May we suggest the child knows the man far better than he imagines, doesn't he? The child has a notion far superior than the man about what the man really needs to feel in the world of work, to feel able to manifest who he truly needs to manifest. And in some ways the child is able to tell the man why he cannot manifest himself truly in the way he is working right now, can't he?*

*What can the child tell the man about his attitude to his workplace and the way in which he is able to manifest who he truly is in a world, where work must now become a very different commodity to the one it has been for so long now that no one can imagine it to look any different?*

We feel the way forward, in terms of the attitude to working, needs to take into consideration the attitude to the Self who is working. May we suggest the most significant aspect of the working world today is to enjoy working in a different way to the way we perceive the world enjoying work until now.

May we suggest that if all the people at work in the world were to tell us their motivation for work, first and foremost it would be for the money; whoever we spoke to at the highest level of enjoyment there would still be the 'money' factor because the bills have to be paid first and foremost.

However in our view what money means is the means to undermine the aspect of pleasure in a particularly pernicious manner, and we see the future of money to be precarious at best and therefore the idea of pleasure has to be reperceived as the number one project of work.

Now, what is pleasure? What is enjoyment at the fundamental level of human nature? May we suggest pleasure is in truly being who we are in the deepest sense of pleasure in the knowledge that we are divine beings in the service of a universal plan that was inspired and devised by the creator God, of whom we know very little right now.

We are but cogs in a vast human chain that began in the annals of time and continues to evolve in the unending story of creation. And yet, as God said, every hair on the head of every individual is unique, noted and loved by that Creator God.

Isn't it time we looked to that vastness of our humanity rather than just to money for work that most of us manage to do throughout our lives? And what is more, when we look to our vastness we also measure up to our idea of what we would dearly love to be in our wildest dreams, and yet feel we can never fulfil because – what? We are less than qualified, we are underpaid, we wish we didn't have to work at all, we feel the Gods are against us ever getting promotion. And so on. What a waste of energy!

So what do we do to become workers for God – and by definition 'paid by God', as it were? No one in the universe would work for God without being paid a good rate for the job, would they? And becoming aware of the super abundant life it is possible to lead – simply by staying where we are, doing what we're doing in the service of a super conductor who does know we're here. Not a bad boss, God.

We feel there is quite a resistance to becoming aware of who we truly are though. Why is that? What is the problem in really committing to a life of such vastness it would almost be impossible to do all the things the vastness offers us; skills we can hardly imagine from the wildest science fiction novels of today? What is stopping us taking a crash course in supernature skills?

What is stopping us is quite simply a lack of self worth. May we explain? In the dim and distant past of time, man was totally open to the universal input in such a way that God and man were united in one magnetic input of experience. One day elements in the universe took control of man's magnetic link to God by detaching several strands of the DNA molecule in order to become more powerful than they really warranted.

May we suggest that in the detaching of the magnetic input, man became subject to control by the astral levels of the universe, creating in him a totally reactive mechanism to the emotional input of the universe. In other words karma began to elicit emotionally reactive personal relationships which has kept man into his emotional body ever since.

What man perceives as relationship therefore, is more the emotional response to karmic history of the planet and the individual. Cause and effect is an electro-magnetic response to withdrawal of the DNA strands millennia ago, and the effect is to keep man prisoner of his emotional life, shackled to cycle after cycle of misery because he simply cannot respond to life any other way.

May we suggest that in time human beings will understand the difference between magnetic and electro-magnetic input from the universe in terms of the way relationship becomes more detached, less emotional than heretofore.

In our view ill-health is the result of emotional deprivation in terms of feeling ill-defined, as it were. Ill-defined in terms of really feeling worthy of a place beside God, when so much reactive material keeps man the prisoner of his own limited vision of humanness.

When man can stop the cycle of emotional reactive response to himself, then the DNA strands will widen and 'grow', in order for man to become once again a magnetic creature who relates to God and man by magnetising life, not responding electrically to life.

Responding electrically allows man to become a dramatist in his own lifetime. Relationships are pulled into the electrical circuitry in order to recycle time and again the same emotional responses to inadequacy. It's as simple as that.

Once that cycle is broken then the world is your oyster because, believe it or not, the world is an oyster. In terms of becoming able now to believe in a God who loves and supports you in times of crisis; without a need to sink back into the person who believed beyond everything else that he wasn't worth the candle – to God or anyone else.

May we show you how electrically induced relationships differ from magnetically inspired ones?

*Take a ball in your right hand for a moment. Play with the ball in terms of rolling it round in your hand, taking it with the left and throwing it back to the right, and so on. Feel the ball bouncing back and forward with the two hands and feel what that bouncing back and forth feels like in your solar plexus. Nice, neat bouncing back and forth feels fine.*

*But jerking, non-rhythmical bouncing feels rather disturbing doesn't it? Try it for a while and get the difference in well-being between the nice even rhythmical bounce and the jerky, indifferent, unbalanced bouncing back and forth. Can you tell the difference?*

*Make a note of the difference between the two ways of bouncing the ball from one hand to the other and then think about it carefully. Is the jerky feeling making you think of how you feel in life?*

*What can you feel in terms of the way the ball was never quite able to meet the need you had to feel in touch with it? A grasping sort of feeling that sent you reeling into a sense of not being able to quite make it?*

*Now feel the other way of bouncing the ball, the calm, rhythmic manner of knowing it was coming right back in the way it went away, back and forth back and forth, so easy to predict, so calm to receive, that in the end you felt quite detached from the outcome of receiving the ball because you knew you would.*

That's the difference between an electrically charged manner and a magnetic manner of receiving the world. Of course it means the magnetically charged world of man isn't dramatic; it doesn't have the highs and lows of the dramatic electrical relationship because the 'charge' isn't opposite to man's natural way, but magnetic to his inherent character of Godliness.

Godliness is a magnetic energetic relationship to life whereby 'all is well and all manner of things shall be well', as Dame Julian of Norwich said so succinctly. All shall be well in the magnetic relationship but man has become so used to it not being well that he can't give up the drama of electrically charged relationship to life – and work.

In our view the real significance of the magnetic relationship to life is to become aware that work is not a directive; it's a pleasurable aspect of life, not directed by the internal relationship of man to his emotional hysteria, but a casual unbounded relationship to life as it unfolds through millennia of experience in relation to God the founder and creator of life.

May we suggest to our reader that in the magnetic relationship to life, life 'arrives' on his doorstep, rather than his own need to escape his mental and emotional deprivations pushing him forward into life – and work.

No one isn't pushed to life – and work – by his emotional deprivation, whatever anyone says about their wonderful childhood. No one has escaped the evolutionary cycle of becoming influenced by emotional responses to deprivation of DNA magnetic input.

But now it will be different, we promise, and it is the sensation of change of this magnitude that is creating fear and chaos in people's minds and hearts right now. If it isn't, it should be! Because the extent of change emerging on the planet right now is immense and the outcome of that change will affect everyone on the planet sooner or later.

To hold on to old habits of work, particularly, will soon prove insupportable and in our view the sooner people become aware that life isn't going to be what it seems very soon, the better. Making sure the life becomes magnetic is what needs to be considered and should be considered, in the very near future.

May we state first and foremost that the changes are nothing to do with more brains, more qualifications and more mental activity. No, the additional DNA will make it far more likely that the brainy ones will find themselves in more trouble than those who have felt insecure through lack of them.

As Jesus said 'the meek will inherit the Earth', quite literally because the meek will find it in their hearts to ask the Earth what needs doing, and in doing so will find themselves able to tune into what to feel about themselves in the process.

May we remind the reader that to become aware of Nature herself is to become aware of the man in Nature, who also has a relationship to the Divine in himself. May we suggest to those who fear they 'may not be good enough at it' that all those who are able to feel Nature with their hearts, not their minds, are good enough to know who they are in this world of men.

What needs to happen now is to understand the nature of the feminine aspect of the Divine which is coming into being now at a faster rate of input than anyone could possibly imagine. In our view the way to put paid to the incessant insecurity of man is to really understand how the feminine in man and in Nature works, because until the feminine is instinctually held in its rightful place, no one can feel what it is like to receive the Divinity of Nature and man.

Receiving, as we have said before, is the key to understanding most of man's dissociation with himself; and in the future, man's instinctive need to <u>know</u> must be replaced by his instinctive nature to <u>receive</u> the Will of God and his own Soul's ability to be endlessly creative, come what may, no matter how well qualified in current paternal thinking.

May we suggest that once man's ability to receive is fully in place there will be a different relationship to work in the world. Developing countries are in dire straits because of man's inhumanity to man primarily. But once man in the West particularly is able to receive information about himself and God in a totally natural manner, then all humanity will be able to receive adequate protection from the vagaries of human intervention in the will of God, which states that all His creatures should be adequately fed, clothed and nourished.

Man's need will turn away from man's greed in such a profound and simple way that no one else in the world need go hungry. By the time the second century of the next millennium turns, man will have within his grasp a New World Order in which multi-national corporations too, will be able to treat the world with integrity and understanding.

May we suggest, however, that we start right now to perceive the way of the New World Order in order to completely rationalise our thinking on how the world works mechanically.

In our view the world is not a machine; it is a divinely inspired dream that manifests from the Will of God. In other words it is the Divine Will in each individual that needs now to be manifest in order to understand how the world works; not the individual will that has been in operation since time immemorial with Divine Rule from a Father God in the heavens.

Now man has come of age, it is God's will to allow his people to become the master of their own destinies in a way that would shock the world if they understood its portent.

It was God's dream to make man in his own image, wasn't it? Now he has agreed to allow man to become God in his own image. What exactly does that mean for the average man in the street?

Average man will no longer ever be average again. Every single human being on the planet will recognise the divine inspiration behind his material being, and act accordingly. It's as simple or as complex as that.

May we suggest the most valuable means of support in the world is to become open to the love of the most beautiful person in the whole wide world – you. May we suggest this may not sound very challenging, but in our view this indeed is the most challenging thing for anyone on the planet to take part in; a love of Self that surpasses all other love indeed.

Only by loving Self can we truly understand the love of others, and indeed, the true nature of loving other people as ourselves. A level of unconditionality in our love for Self is the means we provide for our unconditional love of others.

In our view what needs to happen before anything else is accomplished, in terms of the equality of work, is for each and every person on the planet to establish a relationship to his or herself that satisfies their need to feel worthy of being on the planet.

May we ask the reader to tell us, in bold terms now, what exactly he feels he needs to become a worthy human being? We guarantee it means a certain kind of job or a certain amount of money.

Well by now you should realise that this is absolutely not true in the eyes of God, or anyone else in the universe – except human beings who cannot get up to ground level in terms of valuing themselves as complete, wonderful creatures created by God to be creative in His image.

Let the most important aspect of human interaction be with yourself from now on. No one needs to do things in order to please anyone else in terms of creating an image that is not your own image.

Feeling unworthy creates all manner of uncomfortable situations for others. May we say that an awful lot of people on the planet would not do the good works they do if they had an ounce of self worth worthy of themselves. (More social workers feel unable to value themselves than many other people in less 'worthwhile' jobs.)

But an awful lot more people, if they did value themselves more highly, would be compassionate, interested in others, and be able to help in a way that was far more productive in terms of allowing others to become more worthy human beings. It's a catch-22.

Compassion is a natural birthright of every individual on the planet. Compassion only arrives once the emotionality of unworthiness is tackled head on. The difference between compassion and emotionality is absolute. There is nothing more important than catching the habit of feeling unworthy and nipping it in the bud, instantly.

No one escapes the feeling, but anyone can make the effort to disgard it, provided they have no investment in feeling devalued; which invariably they do. It's a catch-22 again. Lots of life is, and it's up to every individual now to take responsibility to catch the catch in the catch-22!

Make a wish now to be totally inside your Integrity. Integrity is a wonderful word that by-passes the awful word morality. Morality is a moving feast depending on culture, predilection or disposition. Integrity, however, demands a person behave according to the highest principles of their self-regulating consciousness.

An apple has Integrity, doesn't it? It is what it is, in its highest form, regardless of how many blemishes it has which others might consider to be unacceptable. If you take a slice out of the apple, you can see that the sum of its parts is still apple, but not apple as we know it. We are all part of the whole in some way and each slice is important, each slice has the integrity of the apple in its grasp, so to speak.

May we suggest there is work for everyone and a job for very few now. In time the world will recognise that work must become a part of the whole pattern of change in terms of recognising that each individual is a valuable part of the whole of mankind which is in a total state of flux right now.

No one is valueless, and in time there will be a work ethic that includes those whose work does not constitute a job, and that they too can be paid according to their merit of being a member of the human race.

This does not mean there will no longer be rich and poor on the planet, but in being 'poor' there will also be a value derived from a less obvious manner of contributing to the well being of the planet as a whole. No one need feel undervalued when they understand the nature of their <u>work</u> as opposed to their <u>job</u>. Make a decision now to understand your work, rather than prescribe to a notion about the job you 'ought, wish or hanker' to be doing.

May we ask everyone on this journey of self-discovery to decide once and for all that the work they do may not be the work they are 'meant' to be doing. No one yet knows how enormously abundant they can be if they could only change their relationship to the idea of financial reward being the be-all and end-all of a useful, happy life.

Make the decision today to take a look at all the ways the job is not good for you and really seek to understand the ways it is taking you away from an understanding of your fellow men in such a way that there is no inkling of the meaning of life in what you do.

Meaning is all in the work life of human beings. Meaning. Meaning is the beginning of looking towards a life that enriches the Soul as well as the body.

Let the work be the bi-product of a journey towards understanding who the human being is in the scheme of things. Then a magnificent thing happens. God will provide. All you need.

# Chapter Seven

# *WHO DARES WINS*

May we suggest the most important thing to remember in the coming months is to make a decision to change. Make a decision to change anything in your life that isn't absolutely the way you want to live life now.

In other words to completely ditch whatever is not working for you; whether it is a relationship, a job, a mode of behaviour that doesn't fit with who you feel you want to be, etc.

In our view the coming months will be an enormous test of strength for many people to truly unload all the rubbish they have accumulated life after life, and to establish once and for all a viable, simplified, workable mode of behaviour to suit the dwindling resources of the planet Earth.

Dwindling resources are a major problem right now as so many of you understand, but so few people really take on board as their responsibility. May we suggest the reason the world is becoming such a difficult place to be is the reason we have stated; money has become the God of man, instead of a means of exchange, and a means of becoming a meaningful human being on the marvellous evolving planet Earth.

In our view a more viable planet Earth is just a step away from reality; it means the difference between the most enormous planetary upheaval in history, or the unfolding of the Divine plan on Earth. May we tell you what we mean?

In the coming months the planet will become sensitised to the most incredible influx of miasmic energies which, we suggest, will allow all the deepest sores of humanity to be discharged into the ethers once and for all. This means, somehow, that human resistance to change will be totally overshadowed by this outpouring of miasmic discharge into the ethers.

In our view this discharging of all miasmas into the ethers will purify the air to such an extent that man will be unable to bear the purification unless his own being has been purified by his own discharge of miasmic history. In other words it is time for every human being on the planet to begin to take responsibility for his own unhappiness.

In some ways it is unhappiness that purveys the air now and creates such a disastrous unfolding of etheric grief that man turns to crime, sexual abuse, disorders of the nervous system and loneliness.

Loneliness is one of the greatest purveyors of grief today; loneliness of spiritual rejection that leads man to believe he has the inalienable right to do what his instincts tell him to, causing grief to others beyond measure.

May we suggest the reason man is so disturbed today is that he has disconnected his instincts from his spirituality in such a way that he cannot become a spiritual being without now detaching the instinctual level of his being from his body because his fear is so overridingly in control.

Fear is the most insidious part of man's nature. Fear of being out of control, of becoming insipid in the eyes of others if he were to let go fear and become a simple, unaffected, loving human being whose needs are in fact quite simple – compared to the way the fear makes him believe he needs more and more and more to become worthwhile in the eyes of other people who also judge their worth on accumulation of more.

Right now the Earth is in a phase of complete overhaul, as it were, in order to align to the great phase of universal change that will allow man to become a spiritualised being in league with the universal mind.

May we suggest to those avid users of the Internet that in fact this is only a symptom of what, in our view, is the purpose of recognising the validity of total coverage of landbased information systems. In other words 'you ain't seen nothing yet'.

The Internet is a metaphor for the incredible spread of information that will be possible, mind to mind, once the universal mind is encompassed into the message switching system of the human body. May we suggest that in the coming decades the Internet will be made redundant, in terms of becoming the means by which information is decoded and spread across the planet.

In the near future it is man himself who will become the instrument of change, who will facilitate the spread of information you could not imagine to exist in the human mind. Information technology is the outcome of the need for man to extend himself beyond his own boundaries and to spread the news of his manner of using information to create an equality of access to all the information there is on the planet.

In future it is man who will access that information from sources beyond our wildest imaginings and release it to anyone who can hear it as a valid and contributory means to a better world view.

In our view what man can do is beyond the wildest dreams of any one politician, economist or banker. It is beyond the wildest dreams of anyone who does not accept that man is far far more than a brain or a money earning piece of machinery. Man is man in God's image, and God's imagination is infinite.

May we suggest that in the near future man will become a

transmitter of such glorious energies that in some ways he will not be able to recognise himself as man, because until now man has been the repository of God's woundedness as well as His achievements. Now, however, as man is able to release those wounds inside his own being, the Godness of man will become far more apparent to the mind's eye.

What is more valuable right now, however, is to recognise the dimly felt reality that fear is the basis of all human weakness and insecurity – that most insidious of all human emotions. Now, though, there is the possibility to change the nature of human fear by releasing all miasmic discharge into the ethers and respond to life with fearlessness and dignity. May we show you what we mean?

### Exercise 6 on tape

*Make a corner of your house your imaginary garden, right now. Take the corner of the garden that most represents 'the peace that passeth all understanding' for you in your garden; a spot that feels possible to describe as peaceful.*

*In the spot you have chosen take a rug to sit down on, and make a decision to really begin to feel the peace in the corner you have chosen. Really feel a sense of peace descending onto your chosen corner of the garden. Feel the way it makes the heart slow down now into a rhythm of contented motion.*

*Feel the heart become a beacon of peace in your body now and allow that feeling of peacefulness to penetrate further; up and along and down and around the body, emanating from the heart that is mirroring the peace and stability of the spot you have chosen, working in rhythm with that place you are now sitting down in.*

*Make the decision now to feel a little dis-ease creeping into the* body. It starts in the solar plexus, we suggest. It makes you feel a little alarmed in some way because some fear is making you feel uneasy after all.

Let the feeling of dis-ease gradually make your whole body begin to curl up into a ball and make you feel you want to hide like a child might want to hide, by creating himself into a small ball that cannot be seen or hurt.

What is that feeling about? What is your fear about? What does that fear make you feel inside; to be curled up like a ball inside and feeling uncomfortable, insecure, really frightened to come out of the ball you have curled into? What is the fear you fear most right now? What is that fear about? Find it inside to describe to yourself what that fear is about now.

And now, when you have discovered the deepest fear inside yourself in your curled up ball, feel a person beside you who tells you not to be afraid. Who is that person? Is it mother or father or someone else?

See who it is, feel who it is, feel who is able to comfort you when you feel so frightened you cannot uncurl from your ball.

How do they help; what do they say or do, or make obvious to you in order to comfort you in your fearful state? Is it a statement about you or a comforting word about the thing you are afraid of? Feel what it is that is making you feel reassured; making you feel less and less afraid as the person is able to tell you, or show you, something that makes you feel better now.

Feel yourself uncurling in renewed comfort and strength now and allow that person who comforted you to go now. See who it was and allow yourself to trust that if ever you are in the situation again you do have someone in your inner being to comfort you and bring you back into a position of strength again.

*Make the decision now to return to that sense of peace and fulfilment the garden created for you in the beginning, and allow yourself to really trust that this peace is a mode of existence that you can have at any moment of your life; at any time you need to feel the peace of love and life and healing.*

In our view what needs to happen in the coming years is an acceptance that the world view will change beyond comprehension at this moment in time. The view that the European Union is unacceptable because a federal Europe simply takes away the individual nation state beyond the reach of each country involved, will simply fade away. What we feel is the most important aspect of a united Europe is the counter balance to a united China.

Once China becomes the most influential economic state in the world there will be a need to counterbalance that with another trading block that competes on equal terms with China. In other words, there will be a complete about turn in order for Europe to actually take on the might of China in the economic arena.

What we want to point out is that it will be imperative for the world to understand China's inner state of being if there is to be a peaceable world view that can accommodate the coming changes on the planet.

What we mean by this is that China has the capacity to include all its disparate states in a way that Europe simply has no access to. Inside China is a mechanism that allows the nation state to succumb to the overall Chineseness of the situation in which they find themselves included. There is an ability in China to absorb and adapt cultural differences that Europe, in its quest for the individual, cannot at present achieve.

May we suggest that in the coming decades a need will arise for Europe to recognise the threat of China in such a way that it will find a way to accept the idea of a European identity that will achieve the most incredible homogeneity of cultural identity, in order to accept the idea of a nation state that submits itself to the overall culture of a national Europe.

May we suggest something that no one seems to have considered? Unless there is a united Europe there will be no United Nations because in time there would be a polarisation between America and China that is potentially the most explosive situation mankind has ever witnessed. Europe needs an overall identity in order to counteract the growing tension between America and China.

Within a short space of time the two unities will find a means to co-operate in the culture of a world view that will take much from each side, so to speak. Neither China nor Europe has the complete answer to world unity, but the comprehension of what each can provide will ease the transition in a New World Order that takes into account the individual (the gift of Europe) and the State (the gift of China) in a totally new way.

*   *   *

Each individual will realise his divinity in such a way that he knows the need for his Soul's well being, rather than the greed of his grasping personality. Need and Greed are the secret metaphors for the right and wrong way to establish a New World Order.

Man has only to establish, through the sense of his well-being, what his needs truly are to realise that in fact all one's needs can be met in such a way that would surprise anyone who still needs to set his sights ever higher in the scale of acquisitions. May we show you what we mean?

*In our view there is an optimum number of people on the planet right now. In the developed countries there is a need to distinguish between the way people choose to live because of their greed and the way they choose to live because they know it suits their needs. In that way there will be far more resources left for those who simply cannot survive in the conditions they are faced with in the developing world.*

*May we suggest the reader takes a pen and writes down in two columns what he feels he absolutely cannot do without in one column and leaves the second blank for the moment. Really eliminate everything you realise you could do without in your life. Ten pints of beer is excessive for anyone. Maybe two or three a week is possible?*

*What does the most important thing to you feel like if you were to have less of it each week? Make a list of things that make you feel very happy to have or do, and feel into each thing carefully as you write it down.*

*Now make a decision which of those things you <u>could</u> do without completely. May we suggest a way to do this, is to put each item on your 'can't do without' list into the solar plexus for a moment.*

*Become aware of the effect this item has on your body for a moment, by concentrating very hard on the item in question and really getting a sense in the body, around the stomach area, what this thing means to you.*

*May we suggest you will be incredibly surprised what the body feels compared to what your mind thinks about all the things you feel totally incomplete without. Some of these items may actually make you feel iller than you need to feel.*

*Some of these items will make you feel very sad to be without and of course you must retain them on your list because the one thing reduced greed is not about is making yourself miserable.*

*In fact if you need something it is absolutely vital that you keep it on your list now. May we suggest, however, that you could be very surprised indeed what can be let go of in the most immediate manner.*

*Remember we are looking at the idea that we can make the most of the life we've got and it's no good dreaming of things that are absolutely not possible to acquire. May we suggest too, that if you are able to feel the property or home you already have in this life in your solar plexus, it too will tell you what is your 'need' for your own being to experience and what is your 'greed' level of accommodation.*

*Make the decision to look deeply and honestly at all the items on your list and feel the affect they have on your life right now, for good or ill, and make another note of the things you really, really cannot do without in the second column; a much reduced column we feel, because no one ever needs as much as they think they do in this life. No one.*

*May we suggest you relax in a chair now and find the list in front of you becoming a scenario for a new attitude to life right now. Feel the things you have chosen to be the most significant properties you need in this life and find yourself feeling into those things that you have deemed really important to you.*

*Feel the list becoming a picture of your life in some way; feel a kind of lighter feeling inside as you contemplate the list you have made as the most important things you need to feel complete now. What does that make you feel? Relieved, frightened because there is so little in life that you really need right now? Amazed?*

*Make a picture in your mind of a life with these things apparently making your life complete. Feel a tingle inside now and feel a completeness inside so that this picture feels so nice you wondered how it was ever difficult to let some of the other things go.*

*It is important to really become complete with this shortened list of*

*needs now so that in the next exercise you can see why the list is*
*able to support you in the life you are choosing to lead in the future*
*now.*

In our view there is only <u>more</u> when you have really been able to
consider using less than you are accustomed to; it is a law of the
universe that once you are truly able to let go of something, it is
then you can have it, if it's what you really need!

But to let go of anything is truly the most difficult thing to do
because human nature has been geared into wanting more and
more, not less and less. However, in the way of things, you cannot
actually become aware of having more until there is a true
understanding of wanting less.

What is required in the coming age of a New World View is the
most inordinate level of courage you will ever be asked to commit
to. The level of courage demanded to really look into the ideas we
are presenting is enormous.

To begin to perceive life totally differently to the way you imagined
does take courage, and 'Who Dares Wins'. Because to dare is to
challenge the status quo of all the mores that the political pundits
put forward; that to grow is to want more, and to deliver more
means less and less ability to understand the value of the human
being.

We feel the way to become aware of the amount of courage this
change in perception requires will become apparent in the
following exercise.

*May we suggest you take a moment to reflect on the list again, to*
*really feel a level of okayness with your reduced list of needs now,*
*and become open to the idea that in fact even this list is too much*
*for the future available to the average human being now. Make a*

*decision to allow yourself to really face a challenge today and make a decision to make the exercise a really potent one for you.*

*Now, look at the list again and take the item that is most important to you right now. Feel into your solar plexus to feel which item is the most important to you.*

*We would suggest the item most people consider indispensable is their car. Most people have access to a car and consider it to be the thing they could not possibly do without. So, for sake of argument, shall we take the car?*

*Feel the car in your solar plexus if you can. Make a note of the feeling you have that using a car brings to you. Is it freedom, or usefulness or making a life that seems humdrum more palatable? What is the sense you have about the car right now, in your solar plexus?*

*Now take the car into your heart and feel the way the feeling changes if you can. Let the car become a different sense of self for you in the heart now. What can you feel that is different to the way it felt in the solar plexus?*

*May we suggest that you stop a moment and <u>draw</u> what the two situations do for you in the solar plexus and then in the heart. By drawing, we mean a quick sketch with any kind of pencil or pen to capture the essence of what we mean when we say there will be a slightly different sense of the car in each chakra; the solar plexus and the heart.*

*Feel back into the solar plexus now and tell us how it feels to have drawn two different relationships to the car. Is it feeling lighter and more detached from the car in some way? How more detached? What is the feeling of detachment like suddenly? What can you feel about the car that you didn't feel before? A sort of detachment about the emotional content of the need to have a car, yes?*

*Now relating to the car in this more detached manner, allow yourself to take a ride in the car, in your imagination. What is the feeling about getting in the car and <u>having</u> to drive somewhere?*

*Is it making you feel rather ambivalent towards driving the car to a place you know well and expect to drive to many more times in your life? Where is the car making for on this drive? A family friend, the supermarket, a place that you know and love for a holiday or weekend break? Why is the car so necessary for this drive? What is the ambivalence about, do you feel?*

*In our view there may be a need to do this particular drive but we guarantee there will be a sense that sometimes it isn't really necessary to take the car on that particular journey at all; that perhaps you might go by train or take the car part way, or become aware that it would almost be a relief if you didn't have to go at all.*

Cars are the most emotional issue, after the home you live in, as far as need is concerned. What we are suggesting is that in fact there is less need for huge cars, less need for huge houses, less need for anything if you are able to consider your needs in the light of an inner realisation that need is a very personal, very specific aspect of our lives; and need for one person is not a need for another from the deepest sense of our knowing, rather from the greed of thinking we need what everyone else thinks they need.

*        *        *

May we ask the reader to become open now to the idea that fear cannot be tolerated in a world where life becomes the instigator rather than the follower of fashion. We mean by this that in the coming months and years a real effort needs to be made to feel safe on the planet in the life you have, not always creating a fear base that makes you want to have so much more than you ever need and are ever likely to need. Fear is the opposite of love and in that sense it is daring to love that creates the ability to let go of fear. May we show you what we mean?

Make the decision now that love must be the instigating factor of your life, not fear. Make the decision to really understand how love in the usual sense of the word has been used to create fear because emotionality has been a substitute for real compassion, which is the buzz word of a free, safe world of men now.

Compassion is not emotionality at all. It is a word that encompasses freely, not compresses. May we suggest love is not about imprisoning but about letting go; and in the coming months and years there needs to be a real understanding of our misunderstanding of love in the real sense.

May we show the difference between love emotionally and love compassionately?

### Exercise 7 on tape

*May we suggest you settle down into a nice relaxed state in the seat and really make the effort to take on board the idea that compassion is the way for love to go now, not the emotionality of possessive love which most couples indeed do find themselves perpetuating unconsciously and unwillingly.*

*Now, feel a worm inside your solar plexus. It is wriggling, isn't it, to get air from the Earth's form right now? How do you feel the worm's need for air in the Earth's form? Can you feel the weight of the Earth above the worm and feel the worm creating its own space, creating its own air out of the Earth?*

*Feel that the Earth feels compassionate to the worm's need, doesn't it? In what way is the Earth compassionate to the worm's need? Can you feel the Earth's acceptance of the worm?*

*How is the worm able to make space for itself through the Earth's compassionate nature? The worm takes in the Earth and expels it, doesn't it? Because the Earth is compassionate to its needs. What does that mean, that the Earth is understanding and accepting of the worm? That is what compassion is all about, isn't it?*

*Now feel the worm wriggling in the Earth in some way. And feel another worm wriggling towards it, who loves the worm very very much. So much it feels most indignant that worm is feeling perfectly okay on its own in Earth's compassion.*

*What does worm feel about lady worm in her lovingness towards him; when she doesn't feel he has all he needs already, but needs her to complete his well-being? A lot of resentment? So what does love look like to the worm? Ownership? Neediness?*

*Now be Miss Worm in the situation and feel very happy in Earth's compassionate embrace. But feel a need for Mr Worm's presence. Why do you need Mr Worm to feel loved? Do you not feel complete without Mr Worm? Only half a worm?*

*So let Mr Worm fall in love with Miss Worm and feel how the love of Mr Worm affects Miss Worm suddenly. Does she feel constricted? May we suggest Mr Worm needs to be in control, doesn't he?*

*May we suggest Mr Worm loves to control, and Miss Worm makes Mr Worm feel trapped by neediness. So how do they get out of love that is emotional in this manner? What does Earth offer that neither Miss nor Mr Worm offers? Unconditionality? Holding without controlling? In the last scenario Mr Worm feels safe controlling, and Miss Worm makes Mr Worm take her neediness to great lengths so she feels safe.*

*But if Miss Worm and Mr Worm could just feel safe in the Earth they would be happier together and make little worms; and not make themselves safe through 'love' born of fear, rather than through compassion. Who dares to show compassion wins their freedom to be who they really are, don't they?*

May we suggest that worms are the best example of making the decision to allow each individual to explore their masculine and feminine sides; to experience the integration of both the masculine and feminine aspects of themselves in order to understand how life and love can become a matter of equality and mutuality that creates a compassionate love for freedom of all individuals.

May we ask the reader to really make a conscious choice now to become open to the aspects of themselves that have so far not been able to manifest through fear of feeling unsafe.

There are many many ways to manifest the life everlasting while incarnating on the planet but most of all there comes a time when man needs to recognise that rage overlies fear, and fear is the one aspect of man that can no longer be tolerated if the planet is to become the magnificent place it is meant to be.

**If you feel you are fearful of yourself there will never be a better moment to try to let that fear go, because the sense we have is that the moment of fear is over now.**

We want to reassure all those who are fearful of sinking to the bottom of the ocean, that there is no time like the present to believe that man is a creature of God, and as such there is life everlasting. Life everlasting means that the fear of death is no longer the deepest fear that man has and if man no longer fears death, then there simply is no need for fear.

Diana, Princess of Wales made us recognise that love is the manifest common denominator of every single human being on planet Earth. And we challenge anyone to tell us that they did not at one moment in the aftermath of her tragic death feel 'if Diana can die and leave such a wonderful legacy, then perhaps death is not such a terrible thing after all'. Yes?

Diana was a being of huge personal and collective Light. Her presence on Earth was given to humanity in order to accelerate the human heart at this great transitory moment. Her death made us think about life and death in a new way.

Her legacy lives on in us, in that we may no longer fear death as the great divide, but as the energy that lingers within us to move us into the Great Beyond in which we live and move and have our being.

# Chapter Eight
# *AND SO BE IT*

We would suggest that in the coming months a marvellous opportunity will arise for each person to make a commitment to a more flexible mode of living that will enable each and every one of you to become aware that there is more to the life you have than you could possibly have imagined.

We feel the most important thing to recognise right now is that the planet is becoming far more flexible in and of itself. We mean by this that there is more plasticity in the atmosphere than ever you could imagine, but this plasticity is the result of each individual becoming more open to the inner gaze.

In a very short while there will be more and more opportunity to create from the ethers exactly the kind of future you wish for yourselves, provided the atmosphere in and around you is clear enough for this plasticity to work.

This is why it is vital for each person to take responsibility for their own actions and reactions, because unless you do, not only will you miss out on the adventure of a lifetime, but you will also become a contaminant of the planet as a whole.

Believe us, the emotional pollution of the planet is far more dangerous and 'sticky' than any of the carboniferants being pumped on to the planet by dangerous exhaust fumes.

In fact if the environmental lobby could see how much worse their own emotional junk is than any output from industry in the Eastern Block they might think again about priorities for the coming years.

In our view the most precious commodity anyone can possess is clean air. Not in the sense of making sure every breath you take is filtered and scrubbed from the outside, but from the inside. May we suggest the real problem with the planet is the inability of individuals to experience themselves as human beings.

May we ask anyone on the mailing list of anything at all what their first reaction is to the pile of bumph they receive through the door? We guarantee the first reaction is 'can I afford it? It may be such a fleeting thought that you hardly recognise it to be there, but it is. We guarantee. Can I afford it? Everything is can I afford it? Isn't it?

May we ask what the next question is? Can it make me more able to make my way in the world? What will it do for my status? No? Think hard. What is the motive for most of your exploits in the world now? To get on. To get ahead. Depending on the sort of upbringing you had, this need to 'get on' is lurking further from, or nearer to, the surface of your being. 'Getting on' is the motivation for all the striving in the world today.

But what if the human being has a different motive for his life from now on. What if we were to suggest that in our view there is another motive that the human being was 'meant' to be pursuing in life? What if we were to suggest the most important pursuit for the evolved human being is to really make the grade as a human being now?

And that means being pure and clean inside; free as air from the pollution of the emotional body that is actually beginning to break up in the atmosphere as the cleansing and clearing of many individuals goes on apace, threatening to leave many other people who are still motivated by 'getting on' far behind. 'The meek shall inherit the Earth'. We say it again.

We feel the real issue at stake here is to make the assumption that a real shift is happening on the planet which will make it quite difficult for each individual to continue the way of doing things that has carried him through the last ten thousand years!

May we suggest that in the coming months and years a very new atmosphere is surrounding the Earth which will preclude the old ways of being from succeeding any more. Like atmospheres of other planets are inhospitable to the form of life you are constantly looking for, so the Earth herself will also become too rarefied for most people to survive on, unless they have clarified their human status rather than their social or political one.

May we suggest the way forward might be to watch the process that takes place when you do things only to get on, to succeed in life beyond all other motivations.

### Exercise 8 on tape

*Form a small circle inside the solar plexus. Make it a blue circle that you can step inside if you feel you need to retreat.*

*Now make a more spacious circle around you by putting cushions around you in as wide a circle as feels right to you at this particular moment.*

*Make the circle comfortable to yourself. Feel the safety inside the circle and make a note to yourself of how it feels to feel safe now, on the inside. Now really feel safe inside by imagining all the doors of your house are open, all the windows and inlets are wide open, so that under normal circumstances you would feel very exposed indeed, and then return to feeling safe in the circle none the less.*

*Now wait a moment in the circle, and then return to the inner circle in your solar plexus. What does that make you feel, to sense the inner blue light circle in the solar plexus right now? Feel the way the inner circle is holding you absolutely inside yourself, even more securely than you felt in the wider circle.*

*Make a real effort to consider this inner circle your harem circle; in other words this is where the most precious parts of your being can safely harbour when things get tough in the exercise. Let us begin.*

*Feel a very big man in the outer circle with you now. Feel the way this man wants you to feel insecure inside because he is such a big guy and you are such a small fry in his terms. Feel the way you sink down inside yourself when he walks towards you swinging his arms, confidently and unashamedly showing you how very magnificent he is in the scheme of things.*

*Wait for him to reach you and recognise as he stands in front of you a person who is actually quite familiar to you. Feel his familiarity in some way by looking hard at his arms, his legs, his massive chest, etc.*

*In your looking hard at this giant man in front of you, become aware that your heart is pounding a little because he makes you feel like you want to be big like this man in front of you. Make a gesture to yourself in the circle that, yes, I want to look like this man, all confidence and striding towards people in this manner.*

*Make your gesture to yourself and tell yourself how it feels to want to be a big man suddenly. Feel what it feels like to say, I want to be big like this man. Now tell yourself, well, yes, I can be like this big man, can't I? Feel what that recognition feels like. What does it mean to say, hum, that's me, that big man is me now?*

*Take a second to feel what's happening inside when you tell yourself you can become as big a man as this. Feel what happens to your well-being suddenly. Be aware that in wanting to become this big man there is a shift in the way you feel secure in your circle. Can you feel that shift?*

*What is happening in your circle as you become convinced you can become this big man? Sense the panic that begins to happen inside your circle, at the same time feeling the increasing feelings that yes you can become a big man.*

*Now return to the big man in front of you. What can you see in the big man that really appeals to you? Is he able to make others feel insignificant? Can he make you feel insignificant? What does his bigness make you want for yourself? Write this down on a piece of paper now and look at the things you want as a big man.*

*Return to the circle and again check what you feel in the circle, now you have allied yourself to wanting to be that big man being. There is absolutely no safety whatsoever, is there? Why not?*

*Because you have extended yourself beyond the confines of your own being, in wanting to be someone other than who you are; to want to be bigger than you are makes you leak over your circle boundary and disappear into the hinterland of insecurity, doesn't it?*

*Remain in your circle, on a chair, if you like. Reach down inside yourself to feel the inner circle in the solar plexus. This should still be pretty safe in terms of not being influenced by the man in your outer circle. Let the panic subside again and really feel the peace of your inner circle. Make it so safe that in fact you feel unable to come outside, even though that man is still in the outer circle with you.*

*Make sure the man doesn't encroach on your inner circle, because there needs to be a safe space from prying eyes – which that man now seems to have had. He was prying into your being in such a way that he wouldn't let you go about your normal daily business, would he?*

*Stay safely away from him and become aware that in fact in the circle of safety inside you, you don' t actually like that man at all; he's far to bullying and intrusive on your peace of mind, isn't he?*

*Take a moment to reflect what he made you feel and want to do in your life. Really reflect on his bullying tactics to make you discontent with your lot because he was so much bigger than you were. He persecuted you to want to become something you knew you were not, didn't he?*

*Make a quick assessment of the way he began to make you feel you needed to become a big man too, which in some ways, particularly now in your safe inner circle, you realise was pretty stupid. Why was it stupid?*

*Feel the safety of the inner circle and its aspect to the outer circle. What part of you feels the big man was only tempting you beyond your needs and wishes?*

*May we suggest that in fact you feel pretty good in your safe circle and have no wish at all to become the big man. And yet we feel you do know you can become more and more and more who you are, without becoming so big you go beyond your safety barrier into a panic land – where you need to keep growing bigger and bigger to run away from the panicking that growing bigger brought to you in the first place.*

May we suggest the real issue now is to become aware of the dynamic of plasticity before you moan on that it is all very well not to have a 'getting on' mentality. But how do you earn a living to keep up the mortgage and the payments on the house?

Remember there was a real recognition earlier that 'needs' are very different to 'wants'. To begin with there will be a great need to reduce what you feel you 'ought' to have in terms of the goods and services you think you need, but don't.

But there will always be the need for money exchanges in the world, despite many attempts to return to bargaining. This can be highly successful, and needs to be extended in situations of co-operative living which do become possible in many rural locations, particularly. There is every hope for mankind that a return to barter for those who have something practical to offer others, which can be extended to include many more people than at present believe possible.

However, for those who need to earn a living in the normal sense of the word, there will become a far less rigid relationship to how you choose to do that. There will, of course, always be lawyers and policemen and people who do the daily round of everyday work.

But in our view there will be far more people who decide simply to unfold their potential into areas they could hardly have imagined possible from their school curriculum days and who will influence the world by their innate ability to draw in the exact amount of financial reward to fit their, admittedly restricted, needs base.

There will be many more people who are truly at peace in their smaller lifestyles, who will benefit enormously from a down-shifting of needs. They will be the pioneers of a totally new shift in consciousness that to earn is to be far less mature than to be a person who can draw his salary simply by operating out of his innate creativity.

May we show you how this plasticity works and how to draw as if from the ethers, sufficient capital to do everything you truly know you need to do – and that includes trips abroad, should you still recognise your need to do that?

Needs based plasticity is simply the art of drawing to you the energy you are putting out, in terms of financial reward. There is a direct relation between what you 'show' to the world in your new spiritual domain and what you receive from the world, as your drawing power manifests in terms of creating what you need to become totally self-sufficient and interestingly placed in the world. May we show you what we mean?

*Exercise 9 on tape (you will need a pen and paper for this exercise)*

*Make a small mark with the pen on the piece of paper in front of you. Now let yourself become aware that the mark on the paper wants to extend and grow and become more and more of a mark on the paper. May we suggest this mark becomes a moving marker of yourself now, by releasing a flourish here and there; a flourish of creativity and dynamic intercourse with the paper you are drawing on.*

*Create a mark of such creativity that you begin to feel yourself becoming involved with your mark as you flourish and change and become the guider of your mark rather than the maker of your mark. Let the mark 'make itself' in some ways, as you allow yourself to be the guide and instigator, rather than the maker of the mark.*

*There will be a sense that the mark begins to have a life of its own, it needs to turn here or there, or become a circle or marker point on the page, or whatever you feel it wants to become. Allow yourself to imagine a place that the mark wants to be seen; a location in the house perhaps, or a place in the market place that you feel you know suddenly somewhere.*

*Let the marker become a being in its own right, in a place that you imagine your marker wants to be. Sense your marker in that place and become aware that this marker is you in this place; a free flowing, growing marker on the page of life in this place.*

*Let that feeling of flow and change and happening become the feeling inside you right now, and allow the marker in you to become aware that inside is a place that the marker you fits perfectly.*

*Feel yourself really making the effort to become a marker inside yourself with the sense that in circumstances you don't understand there is a place inside you that makes the decisions for you, not you that makes the decisions for yourself.*

*Make a concerted effort now to find that place that knows your life inside out and knows exactly what it takes to make you feel well, alive, happy and vigorous in the world.*

*This place is the centre of your Soul and is in fact the seat of all your history on the planet since time immemorial and the seat of all that you ever were in the history of time.*

*There is a seat in the marker place that will guide and direct you towards all the money you need. Make a decision now to connect with that place and feel the quality of that seat of the Soul being inside.*

*There will be a moment of reluctance to find that place because it will change the entire focus of your life in one foul swoop. Make a decision now to let that focus be changed because at last there will be a sense of peace and passion that cannot be released until you know for yourself that this is the place you want to be from now on.*

*It will shock and disturb you to know your life has been led under false pretences, but it will shock you too to recognise how simple it all is. What do you need to do to get money for the things you need in this life? That is the question.*

*Make the decision to know what it is you need to do to have enough money for all the things you need in your life. Tell the world in one sentence what that might be. Tell yourself in one gesture what that might be.*

May we suggest that in the very near future the world will become a place that cannot sustain what until now has been the most incredible place of making money hand over fist for those who have made making money their priority in life.

What we want to instil in the reader is an attitude of mind that says, 'what I have is what I need, and if I need more I will manage to draw it to me in the near future because I am waiting on the will of my Soul and of God'.

What needs to be understood is that God is a manner of becoming in the world, not a judgmental God on high who decides who is, or is not, worthy of making money. What we want to manifest in this book is a sense of the wonder of mankind who can manufacture his own destiny in ways he could not comprehend only ten years ago.

The world is becoming a biosphere of incredible proportions which makes the most simple task a task of such wonder and procreation that man himself will realise what a magnificent creature he is becoming on Earth.

When material considerations are the only important factors in a life, then the wondrousness of man is completely undermined. When the wondrousness of man is the prime consideration, money will take care of itself. It's as simple as that.

We feel the way the world works will begin to dawn on more and more people over the coming decade, with of course, the downside of chaos and change that all profound shifts require. No one will feel unaffected by the causal nature of the shift underway in the universe, as well as on planet Earth.

Man is in for the most amazing ride of his lifetime, of any lifetime and many many people know or suspect this from a deep well of knowing inside their beings.

Many people have for several years been aware that the dawn of a New Age has been creeping up on them, demanding their attention in ways that have felt like a terrific sacrifice of their time and their well-being.

However, deep down they know that they have been preparing for the most glorious revolution in history; a peaceful, unfolding plan of consciousness that means the world will discover its true humanity within the coming years in such a way that will become obvious as more and more people recognise their true worth.

No one knows more than the dispossessed, the homeless and the miserable that it's time for a change in dynamic; a change in the terrible rat race of life that has dominated the western culture, particularly since the Industrial Revolution.

Of course we acknowledge and applaud the incredible upliftment of humanity through the industrialisation of the planetary resource base, but now is the hour to recognise that man can and will live in harmony with the Earth who will become a sentient partner in the race towards a lasting and compassionate lifestyle for mankind on Earth.

No one says it's all smooth sailing. No one. There is a hard task ahead for those who need to shift gear into a more aware part of themselves. This requires sacrificing cherished dreams, perhaps, in the recognition that such dreams are the stuff only of dreams in the oncoming wave of energy realignments.

May we ask all of you who say, 'what else is there but to try hard to get on in the world', to take a moment to reflect on the way you feel about those who are not so fortunate to be able to take a view of getting on in the world.

Recognise the instability of the age of hard graft and rich pickings, see the signs in the sleaze allegations; the abuse of so many children in the rage of the age. Parents are angry because they are unfulfilled by whatever they are having to live out in this era of lack of inner clarity.

May we suggest that the imagination is the key to such clarity and no one has understood the full extent of the power of the imagination yet. Once the imagination is used for the truth of the human soul in terms of unfolding human potential creativity, then all will receive – without exception. It's a hard belief to accept, but it's a truth that needs to be made manifest, and fast.

May we suggest that in the coming years of work the most important thing will be to recognise what is happening in the workplace. In some ways there will be more work for some people and less work for those whose skills do not come up to scratch in the normal sense of the current ideal.

Those people who cannot work in the way that they would wish will make the assumption they are not worth a job or will not be considered worthy of becoming a fully paid up member of the human race. Nonsense, nonsense, nonsense.

What we are hoping for those unwaged people is the overwhelming sense that they are part of a bandwagon of change. Make a decision now to take a look at the new mode of becoming human. Make a decision to change what looks like a hopelessness into a starting point for newness. Let's take an example of how to start looking at newness, shall we?

_Exercise 10 on tape_ (you will need a piece of paper for this exercise)

_Make a small hole in a piece of paper. Take the paper in your hand and see the hole in the paper as a chance to look through into a newness of life that is waiting to come into your life right now._

_See the hole as the doorway to a new adventure in time and space because, you know, you can travel into future in some way that may not seem to mean much at first, but is in fact a real clue to how the newness is able to emerge for you in the coming years._

*Look at the hole from a distance at first, and feel how the idea of the future through the other side of the hole feels. Is it an exciting feeling to sense a new life on the other side of that hole?*

*What is the feeling of newness like? What does a future of newness feel like suddenly; almost too much to contemplate, that in fact there might be a new you on the other side of the hole in the paper? Concentrate on that feeling and amplify it with the paper still at a distance.*

*Now bring the paper a little nearer and recognise that your new future is getting closer to you. How is that feeling; how does that alter your perspective on life right now? Is there a sense of excitement that life as you know it will change radically and you'll still be in the world of men, but in a different sense of self?*

*Wait a while to absorb the feelings of the closer future now. Let the paper sort of de-focus as you feel how much a newness is required if your future is to emerge in a different way.*

*Come back to the paper now and feel yourself bringing the hole even closer to your eyes so again it goes out of focus a bit because the hole is so close. What is the sense of newness about? Tell yourself how that newness feels this close, this de-focused closeness to that hole into the future.*

*Now, become aware of someone beside you who can help you truly understand how your newness can be, in a very short while. Ask that it is someone benign and charming and courteous beside you; no one else will do right now. Only a kind, benign and courteous being who is there expressly to help you understand how the newness will feel in the future time of your being.*

*Make a bargain with this being that in the next few moments you will totally believe his or her words of comfort and compassion about how difficult it might be to accept and realign to the newness, but that you will totally trust the feeling that this newness is absolutely what you want to achieve.*

*Make a decision that he or she is absolutely right in what they say to you and that for this moment only you will hear what they have to say about your ability to become a new person in your own right who can now help others to become who they need to be to feel worthy in their own right on planet Earth.*

*Now, feeling the benign being at your side, take the paper right up to your nose and look through the hole in the page. Look through the hole and now, right now, tell yourself how you feel.*

*Looking through that hole, tell yourself how it feels to be witnessing the newness of a person who feels well and happy and comfortable in his own futureness. Do it. Feel it.*

*Allow yourself to really feel how it works; this futureness, this newness. Is it good? Is it comfortable?*

*Is it YOU? Really YOU? Go on, risk being really, really YOU.*

*AT LAST. AT LAST. AT LAST.*

*AND SO BE IT.*

Annie Wilson offers 'Soul Wound' and other workshops, developing themes contained within the book throughout the year in Westbury, Wiltshire and other venues. If you would like further information, please write to:

Rowan Communications Ltd, Fourways, Chalford,
Westbury, Wilts, BA13 3RE.
Fax: UK (01373) 827988
e-mail 100755.2770@compuserve.com